THIN PLACES

6 POSTURES FOR CREATING & PRACTICING MISSIONAL COMMUNITY

JON HUCKINS w/ ROB YACKLEY

the HOUSE studio

The House Studio
PO Box 419527
Kansas City, MO 64141

ISBN 978-0-8341-2887-3
Printed in the United States of America

Editor: Kristen Allen
Cover Design: Arthur Cherry
Interior Design: Sharon Page

www.thehousestudio.com

10 9 8 7 6 5 4 3 2 1

Contents

FOREWORD

When I first met Jon Huckins in the spring of 2007, he was a confident and fresh-faced youth pastor working in a suburban congregation along the California coast. Aside from his uncanny resemblance to the popular comedic actor Owen Wilson, what first struck me about him was his earnest curiosity. We quickly became friends, and he and his wife, Jan, visited our little community in San Francisco to participate in some of our early rhythms and practices. Once, they even brought a group of high school students up for a week to listen, learn, and serve in our neighborhood with us.

With all of Jon's talent as a pastor, I was impressed when he and Jan decided to leave their church work to pursue a vision of becoming part of neighborhood-based intentional Christian community. Over the years I've encountered many young leaders and seminary students who have starry-eyed visions of living a more "missional" and communal life. What is more rare is to see someone actually count the costs, take the risks, and make the transitions necessary to embody that vision as a way of life. Jon and Jan have had the courage to do just that, and I'm amazed by who they are becoming and where this journey has taken them over the past five years.

I'd like to think I had a small part to play in Jon and Jan's eventual connection to NieuCommunities (since I set them up to stay with good friends in London, who introduced them to Rob and Laurie Yackley). Sometime in 2005, over a delicious Thai lunch in my neighborhood, Rob Yackley and I met to compare notes on our common efforts to create missional-monastic communities. What I appreciate about NieuCommunities, and what I think is their unique contribution to a wider movement, is their ability to translate the best of a missional perspective into tangible and replicable paths of formation. NieuCommunities and a growing movement of communities across the globe are discovering that real life and real transformation happen in the context of intentional practices and authentic relationships.

In the fall of 2011, my wife, Lisa, and I had the opportunity to visit NieuCommunities San Diego, and it was inspiring to meet the vibrant community of people described in this book. We saw firsthand their thoughtful approach to leader formation and the creative ways they have rooted themselves in a particular neighborhood. Deeply committed to their mission and to one another, they also know how to laugh, play, and have fun.

Reading *Thin Places* took me back to the vision of the gospel, the church, and the stories of saints that have animated my own journey. The Introduction to the book is a remarkably clear and concise description of an emerging missional perspective that has developed over recent years. So many of Jon's and NieuCommunities' conversation subjects have been my own. But even more, I've experienced the transformational potency and been shaped by the postures of apprenticeship to Jesus described in these pages.

In this book, Jon Huckins paints a beautiful picture of what can happen when a group of people, rooted in a particular place, seek a way of life in Jesus together. I hope this book inspires many to take new risks to practice the way of Jesus in their local contexts. While I'm hopeful about the possibilities, I'm also painfully aware of the cultural captivity that might prevent us from experiencing the fruitful vitality promised by Jesus and described in these pages. In his well-known parable of the sower, Jesus describes the seed that fell among the thorns, which "'stands for those who hear, but as they go on their way they are choked by life's worries, riches and pleasures, and they do not mature'" (Luke 8:14).

Living in the thin places where we learn to see and participate in God's healing work in our world requires a pace of life that stands in contrast to the individualism, fear, materialism, and self-protection that unconsciously drive American culture. This book is a winsome yet dangerous invitation into a better dream to be awake to all that God is doing in and around us, and to "'learn the unforced rhythms of grace'" (Matthew 11:28, *MSG*). If the vision of the missional church is to be more than mere rhetoric, a passing slogan, or cliché, then we are going to have to figure out how to live more simply and contemplatively, move at a slower pace, get creative about resources and funding, and inhabit deeper paths of local life together.

Together, let's take steps toward the thin places.

Mark Scandrette
Author of *Soul Graffiti* and *Practicing the Way of Jesus* and
Cofounder of ReIMAGINE!
San Francisco, California

PREFACE

NieuCommunities was born in a drafty old barn in the middle of a southern California strawberry field in 2002. It was an unusual place to birth what has become an uncommon collective of missional communities that are now sprinkled in urban settings around the globe. To be honest, though, we didn't set out to do anything unusual or special. We weren't, and still aren't, motivated by a desire to be flashy or conspicuous. We simply wanted to follow God in the way of Jesus and mentor others to do the same. You might even say that we set out to do an old thing once again more than we set out to create a new thing.

When I first pondered the core life practices of Jesus that I hoped would animate our communities as we sought to embody his ways, this short and manifestly oversimplified summary is what I penciled out:

- Jesus lingered long with his Father
- He invited a small band of people to do life with him
- He sent his disciples into the world all around them to be good news

Although we've refined our words and expanded our understanding of them over the years, we've never drifted far from these core practices of Jesus. They have shaped who we are and what we have to offer. They form the framework for the community covenant that holds us together. They sustain and bleed through the missional postures you will read about in this book. If Christ is the cornerstone of the church, then these practices are the practices that lie very near to the corner and are the ones we have architected our communities to build upon.

I would be naïve and less than honest to give the impression that our communities took their first breaths and drew their life solely through the lungs of Jesus. There were other influences at work of which time will only allow me to acknowledge a few.

First, my own experience: I was forty-four years old in 2002, and by then I had lived on both sides of the Iron Curtain and had worked extensively with church leaders and missions teams in over a dozen countries and on five uniquely different continents. My perspective on what it means to truly follow Jesus had been tested, refined, sometimes fractured, and inevitably reshaped by the complexities of cultures and the colliding worldviews I often encountered and wrestled to unravel. These global experiences have certainly influenced—hopefully in an integrating, holistic way—the design of NieuCommunities.

Second, the experiences of other leaders: NieuCommunities was created by a community of leaders, not by an individual. Our co-creators (Phil and Laina Graf, Tim and Ute Warkentin, and Tim and Britany McDonald) and our early leaders (Amy Wilson-Roberts, Bryan and Daleen Ward, and Arthur and Melissa Stewart) also brought diverse experiences and perspectives to the table. They drew their learnings from co-laboring with leaders in contexts that ranged from upscale attractional congregations to Russian youth groups to candlelit emerging churches to gang-banger cells in the barrio. All of those experiences shaped and informed what we have formed.

And finally, we have unmistakably been shaped by a deep desire to form people who will be a gift to a changing world. It has been said that the first job of a leader is to define reality, and the reality we saw was that of a church that was losing its voice in culture and of leaders being trained to form congregations for a world that was passing away…and many of them knew it.

As the calendar was about to roll over into a new millennium, I began to ask leaders across the globe to describe their "dream team"—the kind of people they would need around them in order to relate to and influence their changing contexts. What would they be like? What would they need to know and understand? What should they be ready to do? The most frequent answers to those questions and the responses we found showing up across multiple cultures lie behind the postures presented here.

They didn't come to us overnight nor were they in place when we began. We struggled to get our arms around all that we had heard. We quickly and almost instinctively began to over-educate and under-form our new apprentices. We knew we were burying them in good information more than we were changing their hearts and their life practices.

And so, just months into our pilot community and after a year of preparation, we reached for the pause button. We didn't send anybody home or stop gathering, but we stepped back and asked God to remind us again what we were to be about. Over lots of late night conversations in the barn and countless burritos at a local dive taco shop, we dug hard for the deepest, most essential threads that ran through our overweight curriculum. And then, one afternoon, in the back room of Tomas Café, the thought of the postures came to us, and it came with a sense of divine grace. The idea of the postures resonated with both our spirits and our experience. They offered us a picture of the kind of people we hoped to shape and the journey we often must take to get there. And they offered us a developmental pathway we could actually travel with other people—one that would form us rather than just inform us.

These six missional postures, built on the three practices and commitments we drew from the ways of Jesus, have served us well. If they have made our communities distinctive, it was certainly not by design. We probably could have saved ourselves some sleep and pain if we had been more diligent to learn from communities that had gone before us. That was our mistake. But there is probably no path that will lead to true community that doesn't involve pain. We hope our story and our learnings will lessen the pain (but not free you from it) and encourage you to find your own unique way of shaping people to live in the way of Jesus.

It is at this point that I hand over the telling of our story—and the postures that so intimately fill it out—to Jon Huckins. He is not only a writer, but a leader in our community whose family chooses to give their lives to this way of life. His voice and heart come from the first-person perspective of one who has navigated the waters of missional community—first as an apprentice in NieuCommunities and then as a leader—with a passion to develop leaders and neighborhoods that will enjoy and extend God's loving kingdom.

—Rob Yackley,
Cofounder and lead architect of NieuCommunities

Before we jump in too deep, I want to take a minute to paint a clear picture of the unique context in which I am writing. Also, I will give a brief snapshot of how to best approach this book as you read individually or, ideally, with your community of faith.

NieuCommunities—our collective of missional communities—currently has three sites: Vancouver, British Columbia; Pretoria, South Africa; and San Diego, California. Our vision is not to accumulate large numbers of people at any of our sites, but to empower leaders to multiply other expressions of missional community out of the communities that already exist. Our communities are made up of both our neighbors who have chosen to follow the way of Jesus in the context of our intentional community and of apprentices who have come from all over the globe to live among our tribe for a one-to-two-year apprenticeship of living on mission, being trained and sent as missional leaders.

I currently live and serve as part of the missional community in the neighborhood of Golden Hill, just up the hill from downtown San Diego. You will hear much more about our neighborhood and surrounding context, but it is important to know that all of us who have committed to NieuCommunities:

- Live within a ten-minute walking distance from each other
- Regularly share common meals and everyday life (some even choose to share homes)
- Regularly gather for worship and prayer
- Are committed to live on mission in the local halfway homes, community centers, sports fields, farmers' markets, refugee populations, and so on
- Regularly participate in intentional times of mentoring and coaching

As a way to formalize our mission, each year we sign a covenant that we will commit to commune with God, live in deep community with one another, and extend on mission by diving deeply into the fabric of our local context. It is this commitment to God, each other, and our context that informs our six postures of apprenticeship; they create the context for us to put into practice our covenant to God, each other, and our context.

These are six critical postures that we see in missional leaders and seek to form in people—six postures that have a natural sequence and that tend to follow one another (though not always picture perfectly). These postures build on one another, enabling us to enter into a context and someday leave it having inhabited it well.

It is these postures that form the content of this book. The following six chapters are a brief attempt to unpack our shared pilgrimage through the six postures for creating and practicing missional community. At the end of each chapter, we provide Integrating and Sustaining Practices—concrete practices that we have put in place over the years of navigating missional community. We also offer Missional Possibilities—questions that we hope will spark your imagination for what missional community might look like in the unique soil of your context.

While this book can be read individually and be helpful, it is ideal to be read in the context of community. Our hope is that our attempt at living faithfully to the call of God on our community serves as both an inspiration to explore, imagine, and experiment and as a tangible guide to lived practices that inform the life and practice of missional community.

INTRODUCTION

"It is not the church that has a mission of salvation to fulfill in the world; it is the mission of the Son and the Spirit through the Father that includes the church."[1]

I grew up having a very specific picture of missionaries. I thought all missionaries heroically saved massive numbers of souls in places that no one in their right mind would ever want to live. As a kid, I can remember praying something like, "God, I'm willing to be a missionary, but I really, really don't want to have to live halfway across the world and eat worms for dinner."

Now this elementary, but often common, perception of "the missionary" tells us a lot of things, but I will highlight only a couple pertinent ones. First, my perception of missionaries living in places that no one else would ever want to live is deeply rooted in an ethnocentric reality that has pervaded the Western church: "We" have arrived. We live in the most desirable location, we have all the answers, and it is our responsibility to go tell the rest of the world what to think and how to live. Such ethnocentricity has created a paradigm of mission that has at times been more of a reflection of colonialism than an invitation into the global kingdom of God.

Second, and probably most importantly, this picture tells us something significant about the perceived identity and role of the missionary. The missionary is someone the church sends to go extend the mission of God in some place other than our local context. This inherently means that those of us in the church at home are off the hook. The missionary identity and role are reserved only for those who are called to leave their native country and live lives that no one else would want to live among people with whom no one else would want to interact.

While I am aware I am making some assumptions, I think this image is something we as the Western church have largely bought into as both individuals and faith communities—whether consciously or subconsciously. Such a reality has led to an incomplete and fragmented understanding of the mission of God (*missio Dei*) and our role as active participants on that mission. It is a subconscious understanding that says that somehow the mission of God isn't happening here in our local neighborhoods, cities, or countries . . . or, if it is, we certainly don't need to extend it like it needs to be extended to all "those" people across the world.

But there is much hope.

I was recently attending a service at my childhood church—the same church that instilled in me a fragmented understanding of mission as a child—and as I strolled through the lobby, I noticed something different. Something brilliant. Something hopeful. Something that told me, "There is change afoot, and it is a change that is radically going to fuel the mission of God in new and creative ways."

One wall in the lobby had pictures of all the missionaries who are supported by the church. They were in places like China, Sudan, and Zimbabwe. At first I was transported back to the missionary image of my youth. And then I came to the last missionary picture. But it wasn't a picture. It was a mirror.

The missionary was no longer only the iconic hero halfway across the globe. It was me. It is all of us—in our neighborhoods, schools, families, workplaces. With the presence of this mirror, this church community was saying, "We are not only supporting and sending missionaries across the globe: we are supporting and sending missionaries across the street."

This is the mission of God. A mission to which I now turn my attention.

MISSIO DEI

It has often been assumed that mission is something we do rather than the framing narrative of God in which we participate. In his book, *The Church in the Power of the Spirit: A Contribution to Messianic Ecclesiology,* Jurgen Moltmann says, "It is not the church that has a mission of salvation to fulfill in the world; it is the mission of the Son and the Spirit through the Father that includes the church."[2] When we extend the good news of the kingdom in Jesus, we are not "doing" missions: we are acting as participants in the mission of God, which has been unfolding since the beginning of humanity's story.

In his masterful work, *The Mission of God: Unlocking the Bible's Grand Narrative,* Christopher Wright defines mission as "our committed participation as God's people, at God's invitation and command, in God's own mission within the history of God's world for the redemption of God's creation."[3] So, mission is about what God has done and is doing to extend an invitation of restoration and reconciliation to humanity. God has chosen to commission his people to act as central players in this mission of redemption—players who extend the heart of God to all people in all nations.

Missio Dei is the Latin theological term that simply means the mission of God. Central to the mission of God is the re-gathering of all the cosmos into intimate relationship with himself. The missio Dei is not simply a topic in the Bible that we can cite in an effort to build a rationale for the necessity of doing missionary work.[4] Rather, "the writings that now comprise our Bible are themselves the product of and witness to the mission of God—the whole Bible is itself a 'missional' phenomenon."[5] The narrative from which all the rest of our theology is birthed is that of the missio Dei.

The word "missional" has become a bit of a buzzword in the past few years and has sometimes been used as a brand rather than a dynamic reality that encapsulates the heart of God and his desired vocation for his people. "Missional" is simply a description of a people or movement committed to advancing and participating in the missio Dei. It is a people choosing to extend, engage, and invite others into the story of God.

The narrative of Scripture and the current life of God's people reflect the missional nature of God. We are to be a missional people because we serve a missional God. Put briefly, as we explore much more closely in the chapters that follow, from the moment humanity chose to break relationship with the creator God, God has been faithful in extending the offer of reconciliation to humanity.

God's missional heart is reflected in his seeking out Abraham to lead a movement of people who would represent God's desire of redemption for all nations. This movement took the form of Israel as the Israelites entered a mutual covenant with God to be people who reflected and extended the mission of God to all people by faithfully maintaining a way of life rooted in fidelity to God. Anytime Israel deviated from their role in the missio Dei, God appointed prophets to speak boldly as a needed corrective of and realignment with the mission to which they had committed.

The ultimate reflection of the missional character of God is found in the incarnation of Jesus. Humanity had in many ways gone wrong, but God was unwilling to give up on us. He kept moving toward us on this mission of reconciliation. In Jesus's life, death, resurrection, and enthronement as king of the kingdom, God's restoration project comes to a culmination. God is so passionate about missionally extending into the human neighborhood that he moves into it. That is the meaning of these remarkable words: "The Word became flesh and made his dwelling among us" (John 1:14). In the person of Jesus, the Word literally "tabernacled," or moved into the neighborhood.

Mission is the work of God that the church simply participates in, not the work of the church that we ask God to bless. Jesus commissioned his disciples to join this mission, and the early church sought to faithfully form faith communities that would embody and advance the missio Dei. Two major movements in church history have sought to faithfully embody and participate in the missio Dei. These *monastic* and *missional* movements make up the foundation for the community we have been called to form and are the foundation of our particular faith community.

THE MONASTIC STREAM (INTERNAL FORMATION)

As a grassroots, Spirit-driven movement, the early church thrived under the heavy hand of the Roman Empire during the first three hundred years following Jesus's life and ministry on earth. It was a movement that didn't offer allegiance to Rome and the "divinely" appointed Caesar, but instead offered allegiance to Jesus. However, as Christianity became more widely accepted (the majority of Roman citizens became "Christians" during the fourth-century-reign of Constantine), Christian nominalism began to pervade the church. The unique soil that had given birth to a cruciform faith was reduced to a label that required less and less abandon to the self-sacrificing way of Jesus. Christianity became "the thing to do" rather than the high calling of one submitted to the way of the cross.

It was this context and ecclesial reality that gave birth to monasticism. Of Egyptian ancestry, Anthony was raised in a wealthy Christian family; after a unique conversion experience, he gave all he had to the poor while choosing to pursue a life of asceticism. Withdrawing from society, Anthony spent the next twenty years of his life in an old fort in the mountains, eating and drinking sparingly as he gave his life to devotion of the contemplative life. For him and for many of his contemporaries, the radical call of Jesus to selfless sacrifice had been lost by the majority of the church, and they saw their intentional way of life as a needed corrective.[6]

Anthony is now known as the Father of Monasticism because his way of life attracted disciples and sparked a new movement that served as a critique to a calcifying church structure and commitment-less Christianity. Anthony's fame spread throughout the Empire, and Emperor Constantine and his two sons even took the time and effort to seek out his counsel and prayer.[7]

As the movement developed, it sparked a renewed submission to the radical call of Jesus and took a variety of forms—some much more extreme than others. For example, Simon the Stylite lived on top of a pillar east of Antioch for thirty-six years as he and others like him became known as "athletes of God" through their selfless sacrifice and devotion.[8] In contrast, Pachomus, a fourth-century monastic, thought it best to pursue the monastic life in the context of community and pioneered the development of the monastery. His monastery became so popular that many others were started, and by the end of the fourth century, a developed Pachomian system had been established for the operation of the community.[9]

Along the way, buildings were erected as a way to keep the world away from the cloistered community or monastery. For these monks, the ideal Christian life was not one of direct engagement with the world for the extension of the kingdom, but one of withdrawal out of a desire to be better formed into devoted, self-sacrificing followers of Jesus. Their witness was not through missions or evangelism, but by offering to the rest of the world a countercultural example of devotion.

It was in this context that the monastery became—and largely still remains—primarily an image of spiritual and communal formation rather than missional advancement and engagement. Although there is much more to the early monastic movement, it is this image of the monastery that I want to come back to and build upon for the sake of our conversation.

THE MISSIONAL STREAM (EXTERNAL EXTENSION)

Although the monastery was—and to some degree still is—a place primarily focused on personal and communal formation through a withdrawal from culture, it largely served as the birthplace of the missional movement within church history. St. Patrick and his successors began to plant seeds of the missional DNA within the soil of monasticism and the church in the fifth century.[10] Having been kidnapped and enslaved by the Irish as a youth, Patrick returned home to Britain with a divine conviction to return to Ireland and invite his persecutors into the way of Jesus.

Not content to withdraw from society for the sake of personal formation, Patrick birthed a new form of monastery— what George G. Hunter III terms "monastic communities".[11] Unlike previous monasteries, Patrick's weren't "organized to protest and escape from the materialism of the Roman world and the corruption of the church; the Celtic monasteries were organized to penetrate the pagan world and to extend the church."[12] These communities were committed to spiritual formation—both individually and communally—*and* they were fueled by the missio Dei to be good news in their new and extremely different context. They were what I see as missional-monastic communities.

Throughout our Christian history, the church often struggled to consistently produce missional-monastic communities, communities that were committed to internal formation that directly influenced their external extension and engagement. The institutions often calcified, the monasteries often withdrew at the expense of missional engagement, and missions turned to violent colonialism.

Obviously the news isn't all bad as the Spirit faithfully led and guided the changing church through its dysfunctions as it continues to do today. With that said, I think these paradigms remain a helpful critique and corrective for the church. It is not enough to be purely focused on formation or purely focused on mission. There must be a dynamic interdependence that allows the Spirit to shape and fuel both individuals and communities as they seek to faithfully participate in the missio Dei.

How often do our faith communities amount to little more than Bible studies? Can the Bible be faithfully "studied" if it isn't put into practice in the "classroom" of our neighborhood, city, or world?

In contrast, how often do we go on mission trips where we don't really have any relationship with the people we are seeking to serve or any understanding of the context in which they live? We have plenty of "outreach" programs, but our relationships with God and with neighborhoods are nothing more than a passing wave.

We can neither remain withdrawn from society in our monasteries nor advance on mission without being fueled by the Spirit. So what does it look like to be a missional-monastic community today in the unique soil of our context?

MISSIONAL-MONASTIC COMMUNITY

Where the image of monasticism has historically been that of a culturally removed monastery and the image of "missions" movements have at times been fueled less by the Spirit and more by blind ambition, members of NieuCommunities seek to hold both images in tension and pave a new road forward. Such a road is characterized by what we see as the best of both movements and their valuable contributions to the missio Dei. In the context of neighborhood, we seek to sustain and multiply missional-monastic communities that form apprentices of Jesus through contemplative life in the context of intentional community. At the same time, we seek to develop missional leaders who see all aspects of life as potential birthing places for the extension of the kingdom.

"Following Jesus means being part of the people who are living into the promises of restoration, the people through whom God is on mission to the nations."[13]

In the same way that our God moved into the neighborhood, seeking to invite us into his story of reconciliation, God's people have been commissioned to missionally engage our neighborhoods with the good news of the kingdom—a kingdom whose king was enthroned through selfless sacrifice and suffering.

Put simply, we believe missional-monastic community creates a fertile soil to commune with God, live in deep community with others, and extend the good news of the kingdom in our local contexts. We believe this because we have experienced the richness of this way of life and ministry for ten years, but also because Jesus offered an integrated example of deep community (both with God and others) and mission.

In the Gospel accounts of Jesus's life and ministry, there are three values of paramount importance to communities of people seeking to faithfully participate in the missio Dei. First, Jesus walked with God. He communed with his Father regularly and sought to live out the story God thought best for him. While others caught up on their sleep, Mark lets us know that Jesus always found a way to get time in with the Father: "Very early in the morning, while it was still dark, Jesus got up, left the house and went off to a solitary place, where he prayed" (Mark 1:35). The life and ministry of Jesus were first fueled by his intimate connection with his Father. We call this value *communion*.

Second, Jesus invited others to share in this story. It was not a story or mission that he thought best to embark upon alone. In fact, the very nature of the mission was that of community. God was seeking to restore community with the cosmos, and Jesus's invitation to companions for the journey gives us deeper glimpses into life in the kingdom. It is not a passive form of community, but an extremely intentional form that requires each to give up everything for the sake of others and the mission. When Jesus said, "'Come, follow me'" (Mark 1:17), he wasn't simply inviting people to come to an event. He was inviting them to come and live with him and change the way they live. We call this value *community*.

Finally, Jesus's life and ministry make it clear that the mission is not to be extended only through his life. It is a mission that requires others to advance to the ends of the earth in the generations to come. This reality is made clear in his acts of equipping his disciples through sharing life and sending them as kingdom representatives into their unique contexts. Jesus commissions them to dive deep into their contexts as a sent people fueled by their communion with God and sustained by their commitment to one another in community. Jesus sends us to enflesh good news in our neighborhoods just as he was sent to do: "'As the Father has sent me, I am sending you'" (John 20:21). We call this value *context*.

In the first chapter of Mark's Gospel, all of these values jump out of the story and are deepened and extended in the chapters that follow. While the monastic and missional movements are helpful in framing our place in church history, it is ultimately in the life of Jesus and his commitment to communion, community, and context that we find our framing example of life and ministry. With this model, we daily make our attempt to walk faithfully with Jesus and equip others to do the same in the unique soil of their context.

Through our commitment to engage God in communion, to engage one another in community, and to engage our contexts as the people of God, we have found a way to integrate these often conflicting movements—monastic and missional—in a holistic, life-giving way.

THE NOT-SO-EASY REALITY OF COMMUNITY

NieuCommunities is a covenant community. Each year we reflect on the past, process what we have learned, and begin to look toward another year of living on mission in the context of community and our neighborhood. It is at this time that we renew our covenant to faithfully commune with God, dive deep into community with one another, and extend on mission in our context. It is an extremely big commitment, but it is one that we believe is well worth it. Some of us are single twentysomethings, others of us are married with young kids, while others are more advanced in life and have kids who are married with kids of their own. We are living on mission together, but we are also raising our kids with each other and giving ourselves to others whom we may never have committed to on such an intimate level. Age is not a prerequisite: calling and commitment are prerequisites.

There is much talk of the value of community within the church nowadays. While this is absolutely true, community life can often be idealized and unrealistic. Honestly, the call to commune with

God and live on mission in the context of covenant community is difficult. It has a cost and requires much sacrifice. When things get hard or when we run into conflict, we can't just walk away from each other and "shop" for another faith community. We are in it together, and we have to navigate the often-tumultuous waters with faithfulness and humility. Based on our experiences over the years, I elaborate on how to navigate the waters of covenant community in Chapter 4.

Birthed out of our missional-monastic DNA, our communities are committed to form others as apprentices of Jesus who are committed to a life on mission. Undergirding this commitment to formation is our understanding that we are all apprentices of Jesus. While some are further along in their apprenticeship and carry more leadership responsibility for the development of others, we are all seeking to be like our rabbi, Jesus.

"True Community begins when I stop obsessing about myself long enough to help you walk the road you have before you. Christian community is recognizable in a oneness of purpose and worship that brings glory to God."[14]

Formation and apprenticeship are not unique to our attempt at missional community. Rather, forming and apprenticing must be central to all missional community as each is representative of the way of Jesus. To live in the way of Jesus is to invite, to form, and to practice.

What is unique to our attempt at missional community are the postures of Jesus apprenticeship that were birthed out of our missional-monastic DNA. Seeking to develop missional leaders who are committed to communion with God, community with one another and to their context, we choose to walk through six postures of missional formation each year. The postures inform and give intentionality to our practices while at the same time creating the context for us to employ our practices.

Cloaked in the covering of covenant community, we pilgrimage through each of the following postures as learners and practitioners:

Listening: We desire to be attuned to God, to self, and to our neighborhood.

Submerging: We desire to embody Jesus in our neighborhood while participating in an apprenticing community.

Inviting: We desire to grasp the depth of God's invitation to kingdom life and to become more inviting and invited people while welcoming our neighbors into God's redemptive story.

Contending: We desire to confront the things that hinder the full expression of the kingdom of God, both spiritual and natural, in our community, among our friends and neighbors, and in our city.

Imagining: We desire to discern God's intent on our lives and help shape transformational faith communities.

Entrusting: We desire to entrust people to God and to others, celebrate our deeper understanding of God's call on our lives, and lean confidently into our future.

CHAPTER 1

LISTENING

"Listen privately, silently to the voices that rise up From the pages of books and from your own heart. Be still and listen to the voices that belong To the streambanks and the trees and the open fields. There are songs and sayings that belong to this place, by which it speaks for itself and no other."[1]

Our intentional community in San Diego recently had the opportunity to spend some extended time with a couple from the Bruderhof community. The Bruderhof has roots as far back as World War II, when they fled Germany due to persecution. They now have communities scattered throughout the world. Ascribing to values birthed out of the Radical Reformation and Anabaptist traditions, they seek to live out the life and teachings of Jesus in very tangible ways.[2]

We spent hours sitting on our patios with Daniel and Sarah as we shared stories of life, faith, and dreams. As they described the life to which they have willingly given themselves out of faithfulness to Jesus, we were inspired and enlivened by their devout commitment to God and to one another. While their commitment to life in intentional community calls them to seemingly radical practices (at least when viewed through the lens of an often nominalistic American Christianity) such as a common purse, daily-shared meals, and communal parenting, what most resonated with me was their posture of listening.

In a spirit of radiant humility, they shared with us that it is easy to think we know God's will for our lives when we are trying to discern it from a purely individualistic perspective. They told us, "we [the Bruderhof community] believe that we must discern God's will for our lives through the shared revelation and council of the community to which we have committed."

I am in no way saying that God hasn't or doesn't speak directly to individuals, but I think the Bruderhof community offers an important corrective in our interpretation of discernment. After all, God created us as communal creatures who have historically interacted with God as a collective people rather than as single persons.

How easy is it to say we know God's will for our lives, when in reality we may simply be manifesting our personal agendas? When we seek to listen to God solely as individuals, we deny our communal DNA and deny the structures God has offered his people as they move forward on mission.

"Taken as a whole the Bible asserts that God's program is directed to the bringing into being of community in the highest sense—a reconciled people, living within a renewed creation, and enjoying the presence of their Redeemer."[3]

LISTENING AS A WAY OF ALIGNMENT

It is for these reasons that we enter our first posture of listening in the context of covenant community. As we seek to listen to God, to self, and to our contexts, we do so through the lens of community. Community is the gift God has given each of his followers as we seek to be faithful to our individual vocations and the overall mission of God.

While listening seems like a basic skill that doesn't require much effort to develop, in many ways it has become a lost art. In a world swirling with noise, we can easily find ourselves sucked into endless outlets of communication. Now, more than ever, we need to listen to and yield to the words of scripture: "'Be still, and know that I am God'" (Psalm 46:10).

The Carthusian monks would argue that when we finally do embrace a listening silence, we may encounter the loudest noise of all in our inner beings.[4] Living as a community of Jesus's apprentices who are being formed and seeking to form others, it is imperative for us to enter the path of formation by listening to God through our communities (both intentional and local contexts) and ourselves.

As a missional community seeking to engage our local contexts with the good news of Jesus, we choose to view our neighborhoods and our cities as our classrooms.[5] If we are to be good news, we need to listen to the needs and dreams of our surrounding contexts. For instance, even though we live in San Diego, we consider Tijuana, Mexico part of our city. When viewing our geographical region from a satellite, there is no clear distinction between San Diego and Tijuana. It is basically one big city whose inhabitants are separated by a haunting wall. Each day, thousands of people cross between San Diego and Tijuana to go to work, visit family, and receive basic health services. Without this dance of economic and social interdependence, both neighboring cities would likely collapse.

A significant number of us from NieuCommunities spend a lot of time in Tijuana supporting local leaders who have given their lives to the underserved of the city. Luis is a native Mexican who has become the father of about twenty-five boys who either don't have parents or whose parents don't have the financial means to give their children everything they need. One of the couples in our intentional community, Shaun and Maria, lived in Mexico for twenty-five years. As a native Mexican, Maria had lived her whole life in Mexico and has known Luis since he was a teenager.

Although Shaun and Maria now live in San Diego, they regularly cross the border to come alongside, encourage, and simply listen to our friend.

I recently tagged along with this couple to go see Luis, his family, and all the boys at the home he runs. As we sat in the run-down courtyard, the boys gathered around Luis, who they all inevitably end up calling "Dad," and they gradually warmed up to our presence. I began to ask Luis some questions about his life and ministry, which led to him sharing his frustrations he has had with the North American church's failure to listen well to the people of his city.

He began by reminding us that Tijuana is the most evangelized city in the world. This is largely due to its proximity to the United States and the wealthy churches just on the other side of the border. He continued by sharing that these churches come down to Tijuana on "mission trips" for a week, build a house or run a vacation Bible school, and leave. While he stressed these churches' right motives, he said, "These mission trips have done terrible damage to the church of Tijuana. If they would simply set aside their agendas and listen to the actual needs of my people, they could come alongside us in transformative ways."

Luis went on to make the point that our imperialistic posture of missions has disabled the church of Tijuana as local churches now simply wait for United States churches to come down for a week or two to do the work that the local churches should be equipping their people to do every day. As a result, Mexican leaders sometimes feel both used and debilitated by these forms of mission. Listening to Luis, I was convicted of my personal involvement in this destruction, having led many of these trips myself. More than that, I realized that the United States church has failed to listen, to really hear and understand the people of Tijuana. Luis simply needs someone to sit with him and listen. The church of Tijuana simply needs us to take a few minutes to come alongside them and listen to their needs right where they are. In the same way, we must also be open to hearing from God through our brothers and sisters across the border.

Listening requires humility and trust in the Spirit, but it is also an act of honoring those we come alongside with the good news of Jesus. As people who seek to form apprentices of Jesus, we begin by listening to the voice of God, to the inner workings of our individual souls, and the complex dynamics of our contexts. In each area, we listen through the lens of covenant community. Listening forces us to set aside our own agendas and open ourselves to the work of the Spirit among the community of God.

When we are out of sync with the work of the Spirit, we compromise our participation in the mission of God. The missio Dei requires us to ask, *Where is God at work, and how can I be part of what he is already doing?* While failing to listen can have tragic consequences, being faithful in listening can create a birthplace for the dreams of God to be made manifest in the midst of humanity.

LISTENING TO GOD THROUGH COMMUNITY

The life of faith and practice is a process that requires an open heart to God, which has direct implications for the way we live and participate in the missio Dei. Some describe our journey toward God as a pilgrimage. A pilgrimage is less about the destination and more about the transformation that takes place along the way. It challenges our assumptions, forces us to wade through adversity, and creates space for the divine breath of God to rest upon each of our lives. As followers of Jesus who are committed to live in daily *communion* with God, we choose to walk the path of spiritual pilgrimage. Our pilgrimage is centered in the way of Jesus: his *life*, *death,* and *resurrection*.

As I walked through the labyrinth alongside other people who had committed to the pilgrimage of God's mission and to a community of fellow pilgrims who had given their devotion to this mission, the moment suddenly became a sacred one. We had built the labyrinth in the backyard of a big Victorian home where we gather for our Sunday night community worship time. It was an odd-looking compilation of patio chairs, yarn, duct tape and computer paper, but it represented something much, much more. Something—when understood in this context—sacred.

Our labyrinth was a journey of worship that led to the heart of God and then back toward the realities of life. We assembled a three-fold path that led us in the way of Jesus's death (releasing), life (receiving), and resurrection (integrating). As we entered the first leg of our pilgrimage that night, we prayed through and released our insecurities, distractions, and failures in the same way that Jesus put to death our bondage to sin.

Seeking to fully offer ourselves to our creator as we navigated closer and closer to the heart he desired all of us to receive, we opened ourselves to receive the gift of life that Jesus embodied and invited others to experience. It is in receiving this life that we are filled with hope, peace, conviction, and transformation. Of course, in receiving the life of Jesus, we also fully commit to being willing to give it away.

The final leg on the three-fold path is one that calls us to live fully into the truth of the resurrection. Jesus's resurrection brought life to all of humanity as he took on the vocation of kingship over the newly inaugurated kingdom. We have each been offered the opportunity to experience resurrection—to step into God's story and participate in his kingdom. As we immerse ourselves in this divine union, we commit to living into a new story—a renewed story whose plot is no longer death, but life.

As I examined and prayed during my time on this pilgrimage, I couldn't help but notice the feet of those in front, alongside, and behind me. I was not alone. I was surrounded by a community of pilgrims who had willingly entered into the same journey as I. Walking toward Christ is a beautiful and transformative endeavor, but walking toward Christ as a community of believers is stepping in the very path God has designed for each one of us. With each step, we were saying to God, "We are listening for your voice, and we invite you into our stories. In fact, we will faithfully step into your story as you step into ours."

It is in moments like these that we are listening and communing with God individually and as representatives of our community. But in this posture, we must be willing to listen to the voice of God. When we commune with the creator, we allow his Spirit to transform and move freely through the life of our community as we continually put to death the ways of old, step fully into the mystery and conviction of life in Jesus, and live lives that reflect the transformation of Jesus's resurrection. It is only with the Spirit's leading that we can then set off on the holy pilgrimage of Jesus discipleship as participants in the mission of God.

LISTENING TO SELF THROUGH COMMUNITY: COACHING THAT TRANSFORMS

As a covenant community, NieuCommunities seeks to create space for the Spirit to move in the lives of each of our participants. One of the central ways we have seen this formation and discernment come to life is in the form of coaching. Through personal coaching, we are able to listen to and discern God's imagination and dreams for each of our lives within his advancing kingdom.

Each person who joins our community is committing to living in constant pursuit of God's call on his or her life. One of the central ways we see that call being unearthed is through a coaching relationship. Coaching is less about receiving instruction from another person and more about creating a space for the coach to ask questions that lead to realizing what the Spirit is already putting on our hearts.

This practice parallels the Quaker tradition of clearness committees, which assume God's image has been inscribed on the lives of each person and our job is simply to navigate the waters back to the true identity and destiny each has been given by the Creator. Through the insightful questions of our intentional community and coaching relationships, we begin to catch sight of what God has designed for us from the very beginning of time.

Ultimately, the voice that is often most difficult to identify and listen to is that of our own soul. In a world that is riddled with noise, fast-paced lifestyles, and expectations (both our own and others'), taking the time to listen to what God is saying through the unique design he has placed in each one of us is a forgotten value.

"I must listen for the truths and values at the heart of my own identity, not the standards by which I must live—but the standards by which I cannot help but live if I am living my own life."[6]

We trust that forming church leaders who have a missional DNA in the context of intentional community is more about creating a space to identify what God has already created them for than it is developing new skills and desires from scratch. So much of opening ourselves to the desires of God is simply listening to what he has done and being willing to step faithfully into the identity and passions he has created within us.

LISTENING TO OUR CONTEXT THROUGH COMMUNITY

Listening to those in our contexts (neighborhoods, cities, and so on) requires patience, consistent presence, and eyes and hears that are open to the stories that are being told all around us. In the same way that the church of the United States must do better to listen to the church of Tijuana, the listening posture requires our community to simply be present—both physically and emotionally—to the people, places, and issues that are the realities of our context. Further, we must choose to listen *to* our community and to listen *as* a community.

San Diego is a world of polarizing opposites. One street is home to the rich and famous while the next street is home to the poor and forgotten. One street may be ruled by the ethnic majority while the next is governed by the ethnic minority. Depending on where they choose to explore, visitors to San Diego might be confronted with extreme violence and poverty or be ushered through the secure gates of the isolated and wealthy. As is probably true in your own context, there are multiple stories being told here. As advocates of the kingdom of God, we must put ourselves in contexts that allow us to listen to the myriad stories that are being told.

A BRIDGE THAT CONNECTS TWO WORLDS

The Coronado Bridge offers an incredibly symbolic and tangible picture of the polarizing realities of the multiple narratives that are alive in our city. The bridge is located right in the center of the picturesque San Diego harbor and connects the "island" of Coronado with the mainland coast. Stretching from one piece of land to another, it begins in a neighborhood that is the antithesis of the neighborhood in which it lands.

Known as "the barrio," the mainland end of the bridge begins in the neighborhood of Barrio Logan. The vast majority of this neighborhood's residents are from Mexico, and their rich culture is made clear throughout the streets. Most notably, the base of the Coronado Bridge begins in Chicano Park, which historically was both the heart of Mexican culture and later one of the most violent and volatile locations in San Diego. While there is still sporadic violence in this park, it is also home to some of the most brilliant and powerful graffiti art I have ever seen. The whole base of the bridge is covered in it, and it tells a story of our city that otherwise would never be seen, heard, or understood by the majority of San Diegans. A walk through the park will unveil both the history and modern story of the joy and the struggle of living in a home away from home due to oppressive circumstances.

While their story is told through the art on the bridge, the story of this neighborhood is not well understood by most. In fact, because of its reputation, most people would never drive through it, let alone offer economic support. Every day the wealthy and powerful drive right over this park and many do not even know it's there—let alone know its significance. It is a place of poverty and displacement for those who haven't been accepted or haven't been able to engage with the larger population.

As we live just a few streets from this neighborhood, its reputation spills into ours on a regular basis. In fact, one of our NieuCommunities families recently woke up to the sound of dozens of gunshots in the alley behind their house. When the police came by to pick up the shell casings and secure the area, the police callously remarked, "That's what happens when you live in the ghetto."

Although Golden Hill used to be referred to as "Heroin Hill" and we live adjacent to a neighborhood that has a reputation for gang activity, we don't feel like we live in the "ghetto." This is our home, and we are constantly in awe of what God is doing to renew and restore areas that were once broken. We don't walk the streets in fear, but with hopeful conviction that this is exactly where Jesus is and where he wants us to be.

Much of this assurance has come as a result of our posture of listening, as a community, to our context. We know that there is more to the story of one gang shooting or piece of graffiti art that might not make sense the first time we drive by. There is a rich culture and are many beautiful people surrounding us, and until we listen to their historical stories and the stories they are telling with their lives, we will have no way of submerging deeper into our neighborhood with the good news of Jesus.

FIELD NOTES—NIEUCOMMUNITIES SOUTH AFRICA

How do you begin to listen to a culture with eleven official languages present in a city that also serves as a place of refuge for countless other nations? Each language represents a people with its own unique cultural nuances that create a whirlpool of missional complexities and need. Within our small urban neighborhood, we experience extreme poverty living next door to extreme wealth. White Africans live next to black Africans. Exiles live next to CEOs, and we all share a central park as a place of intersection amid the chaotic rhythms of life. Here our community finds its home.

For nearly a decade, our community has listened intently to the different songs of the South African landscape. We began our journey in the Northern suburbs before a recent move into the heart of the urban center. We have worshiped alongside the refugee and the rich. We have held the hands of the dying and the arms of the champions. Within this mosaic, we have commonly heard one resounding reality: God's kingdom is like a great banquet. The host of the banquet is inviting every perspective from the various corners of the earth to linger together and feast on a new reality together. In this, there is a sense of necessity. Africans find their identity in the group, not in individualism. It's called ubuntu: *I am because you are. We are hearing the voice of a new humanity in the heart of this African capital city, and we are hearing it because we listen hard for it.*

—Joe Reed

I am one of the managers of our local Golden Hill farmers' market. Every week, this event creates a space and time for those in our neighborhood to step out of our individual worlds and step into something that exists for the good of the whole. Further, it creates the call for local business owners and residents to interact and build relationships that lead to authentic sharing of community. However, the majority of our local business owners are Mexicans and are not represented well at our market or in our local council meetings. We are striving to better listen to their individual stories and better understand their cultural norms in an effort to develop a neighborhood identity that truly displays and embraces the diversity of its residents.

With that, I return to the Coronado Bridge. While it begins in Barrio Logan, it ends on the "island" of Coronado, which is home to some of the most expensive pieces of land in Southern California. It wouldn't be a stretch to see the resident of Barrio Logan mowing the lawn of the Coronado resident. There is a polarization that—when given the eyes to see and ears to listen—is shocking. It's not that the residents of Coronado are bad; it's that they are living a different narrative. In fact, we must listen to their stories as much as we listen to those of Barrio Logan and Golden Hill. This bridge represents a bigger story that is being told in our city. A story of poverty and excess standing side by side. A story of races moving away from each other rather than growing closer. A story of complacency that has led to mutual misunderstanding.

Without actively immersing ourselves in these stories, we simply become part of the problem. As advocates of a kingdom that sees no distinction between rich and poor or white and brown, we must stand amid both narratives and humbly listen to stories that may be very different from our own.

Our Integrating and Sustaining Practices

- Listening begins with "abiding with Christ" (see John 15, *NRSV*). So we abide with Christ by:
  - sitting in silence before God as a community.
  - imagining ourselves in the narratives of Scriptures through the ancient practice of *lectio divina.*
  - setting up a labyrinth in our backyard that acts as a communal pilgrimage through Jesus's life, death, and resurrection.
- We study the concept of spiritual pathways so members of the community are in tune with how they hear from God.
- Each person in our community is in a coaching relationship that creates a space to reflect on what they are learning and have it mirrored back to them.
- We intentionally listen to the stories that are being told in our neighborhood by studying its history and the significance of its places, spending time in those places, praying in and over those places, and sharing our observations with each other.
- We attempt to understand the culture of our neighborhood by looking at it through the grid of worldview, values, beliefs, and desires.
- We seek to know and understand the churches in our neighborhood by visiting them and getting to know their people.
- We get to know the other faiths in our neighborhood. For instance, in Vancouver we take a temple walk each year. We visit a Buddhist monastery and Sikh temple in hopes of bet-

ter understanding the history, beliefs, and practices of our neighbors.

Missional Possibilities

1. Re-read this quote: "It is easy to think we know God's will for our lives when we are trying to discern it from a purely individualistic perspective. We believe that we must discern God's will for our lives through the shared revelation and council of the community to which we have committed."

What feelings and questions does this quote evoke?

2. What places in your neighborhood (brainstorm them!) could serve as a "classroom" in which to listen and learn?
3. Respond to this idea: As a covenant community we choose to listen *to* our community and listen *as* a community.

What do you think it takes for a group of people to listen as a community?

Video Questions[7]

1. On the video, Jon says we can only begin to discern what's going on around us after we listen "to what God might be leading us into individually and as a community." He believes that we can "only begin to discern our way forward" as we listen to God and our community. Do you agree or disagree with the statement that we must listen before we do anything else? Why?
2. On the video, Rob says that we must walk into places "gently" and "[unmask] some of the biases that maybe we came to the table with." In doing so, we are able to put aside our agendas

and preconceived notions as we listen to and learn about those with whom we're engaging.

How can listening to God and our community prevent us from confusing "our own personal agendas" with God's will?

CHAPTER 2

SUBMERGING

"We moved into the neighborhood, but do we live life within it?"[1]

I have always lived near the ocean. Some of my favorite and most sacred moments are walking along the coastline with my wife on a relaxing morning or at sunset. The only thing that I love more than walking along this massive body of blue is stepping into it. Whether I'm surfing, snorkeling, or simply swimming, the ocean tells a completely different story when I allow it to surround me.

A body of water that appears tamed by the constructs of the surrounding shorelines becomes a mysterious and vibrant playground for forms of life that I otherwise would never know existed. It is as though I see the ocean for the very first time once I submerge. And ultimately, what I see from below is much more true of its identity than what I see from above as a passive observer.

Much of the same realities are true in our submerging posture. When we give ourselves fully to God, we begin to see and experience the dynamic mystery and identity of one who is inviting us into his story. When we give ourselves to each other, we begin to realize that relationships are designed to be much more than talks about the weather or to be used for personal gain. When we submerge into our context, we see that the story we have been told to believe about our neighbors, politics, and economy is far from reality.

Before we submerge, our perceptions and definitions about God, each other, and our contexts are like looking at the ocean's surface—simple and easy to define because we haven't engaged the mysteries that lie beneath. When we submerge, we are able to encounter and see the way things really are. With these new eyes, we can exchange a god that has been defined for us for a God who is intimately at work in and among us.

When we submerge, we move from being passive observers to active participants. We become residents who are engaged in the deeper realities of our cities and neighborhoods as we find ourselves in the places others may never have seen, experienced, or even known existed.

We find ourselves exactly where Jesus wants us.

REPENTING FROM A PARADIGM OF EXTRACTION

There is much conversation swirling around the attractional versus missional church models. In short (and in what is inevitably an overgeneralization), attractional models pour their time and resources into their worship services so as to create a place to which non-believers will want to come and be exposed to the reality of Jesus. The church campus and/or gathering is the central place or hub to where others are drawn. In contrast, the missional church embraces the mission of God and God's extension into humanity by moving outside the traditional church walls and into the lives of individual non-believers with the hope of introducing them to Jesus in their local context. As such, the focus is not on a central worship gathering, but on equipping believers who are sent to be good news to their neighbors, coworkers, and families.

For the sake of this conversation, I prefer the word extractional over the word attractional when speaking of the traditional, worship-service-centered church structures. First, a missional community is also going to be attractional (albeit in ways much different from that of the former definition) as people are inherently wired for community and are enlivened by shared practices. Second, and most importantly, the traditional church is extractional in the sense that it extracts people from their local contexts to attend a church service and inadvertently teaches us that church is something they go to rather than who they are in the places they inhabit. Many of these people have been taught that attending a church service and serving in it is the central act of our Christian vocation.

Not only does the extractional church sell people short in their understanding of Christian vocation, but it also pulls them out of the contexts in which they live and often disconnects their contribution from their everyday context. Rather than extracting its participants from a place, a missional community is designed to equip its people within a context to enter the stories of those we live alongside. In doing so, we are able to meet people where they are and begin to create a viral movement of embedded followers of Christ who are transforming individuals, communities, neighborhoods, and cities through the power of Jesus.

Living out the submerging posture is the antithesis of the extractional model. When we submerge rather than trying to find ways to draw people into another world, we take it upon ourselves to draw close to our neighbors in contexts that are normative to them. The gospel as Jesus proclaimed it transcends our expectations for where it should be extended and has the potential to come to life in the mundane or unexpected realities of everyday life.

When we submerge, we resist the temptation to drive by the ugly or unglamorous realities of our local context. Instead, led by the power of the Spirit, we pour our time, energy, and heart into the often forgotten places and people with the hopes that the gospel of Jesus might be made real by transforming the realities that envelop us.

A SACRED LIFE BELOW THE SURFACE

As an apprenticing community, we don't simply move to the submerging posture and leave behind the preceding posture of listening. Each posture is designed to build on the one before it. They inform and enhance one another and integrate as one comprehensive attempt to form individuals and communities in the way of Jesus. It is difficult, if not impossible, to submerge well if we haven't first listened well.

I never fully understood the significance of the first thirty years of Jesus's life until I had the opportunity to walk from village to village near the Sea of Galilee in modern-day Israel. Between dusty roads that rise and fall over rolling hills that circle the beautiful body of water, small villages and ancient cities fill out the first-century context of Jesus.

Following the model of his earthly father, Jesus was a carpenter. In that day, carpentry was much more closely associated with rock work than with woodworking. The ancient city of Sepphoris—near Jesus's childhood village of Nazareth—is still largely intact because of the rock structures that served as building foundations Also, because the leaders of the city chose not to participate in the Great Revolt of 66-70 AD against Emperor Vespasian, the Romans didn't destroy the city. In fact, as Herod Antipas (son of Herod the Great) rebuilt the city during the start of the first century, it is likely that Jesus would have spent much time working there as a carpenter.[2]

Sepphoris was a significant city for many reasons. Besides being the Galilean capital, it was the central hub of commerce and a highly influential Jewish place of leadership. There were many layers to life in cities like this and for life in general during the time of Jesus.

As I walked the modern-day ruins of this site, I couldn't help picturing a twenty-year-old Jesus working next to his dad while listening and living a radically submerged life within this context. While shaping rocks that would act as foundations for buildings whose use he may or may not have agreed with, Jesus was present.

Jesus was not just present for a year or two; he was present for thirty years before entering his formal ministry. There is an element of lingering inherent with submerging. It is a willingness to be present to the point of feeling like we are wasting time, when in reality we are leaving ourselves open to being used by the Spirit in ways we be might otherwise have never been aware of. Lingering is not simply walking aimlessly in circles: it is knowing what we are looking for and being intentional with our time and presence.

Jesus, with his building vocation as Messiah and inaugurator of the kingdom of God, spent time to linger, to be fully present and submerge into his context. And he did so for thirty years. Being the one chosen to redeem all of humanity, I have to wonder if he ever felt as thought he was wasting time at any point during the first thirty years of his life. After all, he had a lot of work to do and a renewed story to tell and invite God's people into.

In the end, we know that Jesus wasn't wasting time: he was listening to the voice of his Father and doing the very things he saw his Father doing (see John 5:19). He was submerging deep into his context and preparing to invite others into the story of God. The same is true for us: what may feel like wasted time is quickly redeemed by the Spirit when we linger and submerge with intentionality.

SUBMERGING AND THE STORY OF GOD

Two scriptural stories stand out to me in regard to the submerging posture. The first is of Jesus's baptism in the Jordan by John the Baptist. In what has become one of the most sacred acts in Christian tradition, Jesus's submergence under the surface of the water is an affirmation of Yahweh's submergence into the story of humanity at earlier parts of Scripture. Drawing on the imagery of Yahweh entering the story of the Israelites as he brings them out of and through the water to deliver them from bondage in Egypt, Jesus enters and submerges into the story of humanity with the hope of bringing about redemption and renewal—deliverance.

As followers of Jesus, we accept the vocation to be mediators between God and humanity. We must put to death (act of being submerged in baptism) former identities and agendas and be brought to life (act of being lifted out of the water in baptism) for the sake of the contexts in which we find ourselves.

Another example of this submerging posture comes from the apostle Paul in Acts 17. As one from a Jewish tradition, Paul is found walking the streets of Athens, interacting with local business people and studying the nuances of Greek thought and philosophy. Out of his willingness to listen to his context, to submerge beneath the surface of the mundane, and engage the socio-religious, Paul is able to offer a compelling treatise in Hellenistic language on the authority of God through Jesus.

Living in a time of exile, the prophet Isaiah spoke words of the coming Messiah. Perhaps more importantly though, Jesus the

Messiah often cited the prophet in his teachings. In Isaiah 58, the prophet speaks of the salvation being made real not through fasting or mental ascension, but rather through feeding those in need and through submerging into the lives of those on the fringes of society. In fact, he says, If you do these things, "'your salvation will come like the dawn'" (Isaiah 58:8, *NLT*). And for Isaiah, salvation isn't an escape from reality: it is a radically renewed reality that comes about through the gracious deliverance of a God who desires to restore Israel and all of the cosmos.

Before we can advocate for the hungry and those on the fringes as instructed by the prophet Isaiah and the Messiah Jesus, we must first enter their story. We must submerge.

Ultimately, in Jesus's upside-down kingdom we will encounter the face of Jesus most tangibly when we submerge into the fringes of society.

RADICAL PRESENCE

As we turned the corner we immediately saw Stacey catch the eyes of our daughter, Ruby, and come running down the sidewalk with a huge smile and her arms wide open. Golden Hill is home to seven halfway homes for people recovering from addiction and abuse. In many ways, our neighborhood symbolizes both the brokenness and the hope of restoration.

Stacey is a participant in the CRASH (Community Resources and Self-Help) halfway home, which is a place of recovery for women who have histories of crime and substance abuse. With about four other women who are part of our intentional community, my wife, Jan, has made it a point to enter the story of these hurting women. Whether hosting evenings that give the women a context to share their stories, tutoring classes on computer skills, or walking beside the women during their daily 6:30 a.m. walks through the neighborhood, this band of faithful women has chosen to submerge into the fabric of our neighborhood in the form of these women's lives.

Jan always makes a point to bring our one-year-old daughter, Ruby, along with her when she spends time with the women of CRASH. Many of them have children of their own whom they have had to leave to go through the intense program offered by CRASH. One evening the women in our intentional community hosted a concert and conversation at CRASH. As the women filled a large living room, little Ruby proceeded to dance in the middle as the music played. She crawled around to each woman with a smile on her face and a dance in her step. It was as if each woman was once again being affirmed of their sacredness as ones created in God's image. Through the eyes of a baby, they had no fault, no history, no crime.

Not only is there something sacred about the life of a young child who radiates hope and vitality: releasing the life of that young child into the arms of others is also sacred. As they passed Ruby around, grabbing kisses from her pudgy cheeks, their eyes began to fill with tears as they reflected on their children at home. There was something in the life of Ruby that reminded them of why they were there and gave them hope and motivation to move forward.

It was experiences of radical presence and vulnerability like this one that preceded our interaction on the Saturday morning we walked to the weekly garage sale hosted by CRASH. When Stacey looked into Ruby's eyes and came running to hold her in her arms, she was looking into the eyes of her own three children. Without all the time spent submerging into the stories of these women, an experience like this would not have taken place. Jan's willingness to release Ruby into the arms of those who needed her allowed this precious woman to experience the love that Jesus is pouring out upon her.

As she kissed Ruby's cheeks and spun in circles, I got a glimpse of God's dreams for humanity being made manifest. The kingdom of God was alive and well. It truly was a thin place.

BORDER CROSSING

After graduating from Azusa Pacific University with a Bachelor's degree in youth ministry, David chose to join our NieuCommunities apprenticeship to further integrate his academic learning with everyday life and mission. About a year into David's apprenticeship with our community, he took the submerging posture literally by picking up and moving down to Tijuana to spend a month living with a Mexican family while coming alongside a community of orphaned boys. The boys' home, which is run by a local Christian man named Luis (whom I also mentioned in Chapter 1), is only about twenty-five miles from Golden Hill, but can feel worlds apart.

Driving up steep, dirt hills that are lined by homes of scrap wood, cardboard, and old garage doors, it didn't take long for David to discover the radically different context into which he had chosen to submerge. He quickly realized that submerging in a different country was going to require a complete re-learning of how to listen to both the beautiful and the painful realities of his sister city, Tijuana.

FIELD NOTES: NIEUCOMMUNITIES SOUTH AFRICA

Townships in South Africa are underdeveloped living areas reserved for non-whites, and are most often thought of as a product of apartheid (which means separation). Sadly, segregated townships actually surfaced in the late 1800s, long before apartheid was institutionalized in 1948. However, the system of apartheid utilized and expanded townships to facilitate policies that forced the relocation of people based on race. The history of townships cut a deep divide between the people of South Africa and broke down trust at a fundamental level. This is the history that our team stepped into as we began NieuCommunities in 2003. It was evident from the very beginning that we, as outsiders, had a role to play in helping facilitate reconciliation and healing in a broken land. Our role wasn't grand or well-publicized but personal and neighborly as we acted as a bridge between cultures.

Our black friends in South Africa were often afraid to be in white neighborhoods, and our white Afrikaaner friends and neighbors were equally afraid to step foot in a township. As we submerged into people's lives and made friends on both sides of this cultural divide, we were able to facilitate conversations, a sharing of cultures, and even worship among these groups. As we established deeper relationships with our friends in the townships, people in our community eventually had the opportunity to live with families for short periods of time (and later to actually move into the townships). Sleeping in the same bed, bathing in a bucket, playing soccer in a dirt field, and eating chicken feet for lunch were all part of the experience, but the lasting effect was one of mutual respect and shared life.

Submerging means inviting and accepting invitations to live life together, to be in one another's space, and to step beyond *cultural norms in order to express and establish a new way of kingdom living.*

—Bryan and Daleen Ward

Seeking to fully immerse himself in this new context, David lived with a family who quickly welcomed him as a son and brother. His Mexican "mother," Lily, has a heart to come alongside the poorest of the poor. Naturally, Lily involved David in these relationships, which he describes as shattering his paradigm for the gospel. It was no longer simply a message of salvation from this present life, but it was about bringing hope and new life amid the mundane and seemingly desperate realities of today.

David came from a broken home, and his relationship with his father and understanding of the father-son relationship were shaped by distance and disappointment. But there was something sacred and redemptive in the way his Mexican "father," Alex, chose to approach his relationship with David. The only resource Alex had to offer David was his time. In the everyday activities of going to the grocery store or washing David's truck together, a broken image of family was being restored and redeemed. These moments were emotionally moving for David, but they were also instances in which he saw and experienced Jesus. Although coming from two completely different life stories, God had intimately knit David to this family and begun to heal his deep wounds out of his willingness to fully submerge in a context outside of his comfort zone.

In coming alongside Luis in his work with twenty-five young men who were orphaned or abandoned in their early years, David was captivated by a heart and vision for mission that extended far deeper than anything he had experienced in the States. Carefully shepherding twenty-five young men who are mired in brokenness and insecurity in more ways than are imaginable requires a slow, Spirit-led persistence. Inviting these boys into the ways of Jesus required taking the long way of investing in the hearts and lives of a few to impact many. David discovered that life on mission wasn't glamorous, fast, or an easy seven-step process; rather, it was the intentional submergence and engagement with the people to whom God had called him.

Though he's currently settled back in the States again, David has maintained close relationships with his host family, Luis, and the boys. David reflects on this time as an experience that offered him a context to enter the stories of those who are often on the margins of society and gave him profound clarity and inspiration to pursue his calling to equip the next generation of the global church. He said, "My own borders, crossings, barriers, and prejudices were all broken down. This was part of submerging. I think after all the gunk of my own perceptions was wiped clean, I could see Jesus clearly."

As a community on mission in the context of intentional community, this is often the case. When we extend into the stories of those who are in need of understanding and a voice, we are often the ones taught and given an understanding of who we are and where we fit in the story of God. Submerging cannot be accompanied by thoughts that we are simply trying to go out and save everyone from their problems, but must be done in a posture of humility that acknowledges that we are as much in need of restoration as those we seek to serve.

Submerging in our local contexts opens us up to the wonder and mystery of a God who is constantly wooing his creation and drawing us back to himself. Ultimately, it is only in submerging that we can get a clear picture of the landscape God is using to redeem us and to help us discover our role in it all. Whether in the tear-filled eyes of a mother who is recovering from addiction or in the hopeful but untrusting eyes of a young boy who has been abandoned by the parents who were supposed to love and sustain him, true mission can take place only through the colorful stories of those with whom we intentionally choose to share life.

MAKE GOOD: ENTERING THE WORLD OF ART

Sophia and Jon Hall have a passion for the arts like no others I have ever known. While Jon uses art as a medium for compelling storytelling and teaching, Sophia has the innate ability to turn what looks to be destined for a landfill into brilliant, highly desirable art. As part of our missional community here in Golden Hill, the Halls approach art and the thriving subculture that surrounds it through the lens of social, economic, and relational submergence, asking questions like, *How can we create places where our passions come to life while infusing fresh expressions of sustainability into our local contexts?*

Their answer came a few years ago after Sophia had started what she called the "Handmade Revolution." In short, she acted as an inspiration and host for local artists to display and sell their work every few months right out of Sophia and Jon's living room. Somewhat to their surprise, this idea took off. After over 500 people went through their home one afternoon, they knew they were tapping into something that the neighborhood was passionate about.

Selling only goods that were handmade and "up-cycled" (turning what would have been thrown away into a sellable piece of art), this couple found themselves at the heart of the local art scene with a platform to promote socially responsible products made from the hands of men and women who desperately needed financial stability.

Jon and Sophia ended up opening a store called Make Good that employs local artists who otherwise wouldn't have a context to sell their work. Not only does this store promote kingdom-minded social and economic sustainability: it creates a place for rich relationships to birth forth in our local context. Although part of our missional community, Jon and Sophia are known first as the owners of Make Good in the local art world, and out of that they are able to share the good news of the kingdom through word and deed.

Submerging is not forced. We don't try to push ourselves on people or on our neighborhood. We seek to find places where our passions come to life and embed ourselves deep in those places and those relationships. Whether it is being a consistent presence at the park with a group of fellow mothers, playing basketball every week in the local community center, or gaining a leading voice in the art community, we are a band of Jesus followers who choose to dive deep into the lives and stories of our community with the hope of Jesus.

Our Integrating and Sustaining Practices

We make an intentional effort to eat, shop, and recreate in our own neighborhood.

- We are intentionally present. We walk, we hang out on our porch, and we visit places we normally wouldn't.
- We play in the local community center, we take our kids to the local playgrounds, we play soccer in the park, and we take exercise classes at a local church.
- We volunteer at the neighborhood youth center, we serve at the local recovery homes, and we mentor teenage girls who are looking for big sisters.
- We immerse ourselves in the Gospels and attempt to live below the surface as Jesus did.
- We attend local art exhibits and music shows, and we are present in the overall social and cultural rhythms of our neighborhood.
- In Vancouver, our community spends forty-eight hours every year living homeless and penniless on the streets to better identify with and understand the realities of our neighbors who live on streets.
- Whenever it is possible, we seek employment in our neighborhood even if it means we earn less and have to live more simply.

Missional Possibilities

1. What would you have to learn and change in order to embed yourself into your community? Where would you need to be consistently present?
2. Who are the people around you whom you could naturally get to know? Who are the people outside of your comfort zone whom you can intentionally get to know?
3. What are your hobbies and interests? How can you engage your neighborhood by pursuing your hobbies and interests locally?

Video Questions

1. On the video, Jon says, “We could actually live in a neighborhood but never actually live life within it.” What might it look like to “live life” within your local context?
2. How can Christians who are part of traditional church models still submerge in their neighborhoods?

CHAPTER 3

INVITING

"It is in the shelter of each other that the people live."[1]

Rob had seen his neighbor and son playing baseball in the street many times but hadn't yet had a chance to hear their story or share any of his own. Rob and his wife, Laurie, decided to invite this man and his son over to get to know them better. After an evening of swapping stories around the dinner table that night, the father leaned back and exclaimed, "I just can't believe I'm in your home having a meal. You know, this just doesn't happen anymore. Neighbors don't open their homes like this. Thank you so much." His tone expressed the nervous excitement of one who was unfamiliar with neighborly invitations that lead to generous hospitality and caring interaction.

As we have listened to myriad conversations that our neighborhood has told through its history and present realities, while at the same time submerging into the living rhythms of such places, relationships have begun to form. Practicing the postures of listening and then submerging into our context prepares us to engage the third posture—inviting—with softer hearts and more intimate understanding. In the inviting posture, we learn to tell our stories, tell the story of God, and invite those with whom we have come into relationship into both. People are invited into our lives and faith journey by being welcomed into our homes, small groups, community meals, and worship gatherings.

In this chapter, we explore a posture of missional life and community that seeks to grasp the depth of God's invitation by becoming more inviting people who welcome our neighbors into God's story. We desire to invite others into our lives, but we also hope that because of our willingness to listen and submerge in our neighborhoods, we will be invited into the lives of others.

JESUS'S APPRENTICESHIP

I recently stood on the shores of the Sea of Galilee near where Jesus is thought to have spent much of his adult life in Capernaum. The village is right on the water, and the view of the sea is breathtakingly serene. When standing on the shore looking south, the rolling hills of the ancient Decapolis wrap around the east side of the Galilee, and the city of Tiberias highlights the low hills on the West that lead toward Nazareth. Directly below my feet were the pebbles that led toward the water's edge.

In Jesus's day, the Decapolis would have been a place that represented the gentile Hellenistic culture of the Roman Empire and Tiberias, a place largely espousing Jewish values and tradition. To the north of both, and where I stood on the shores of Galilee, I could picture Jesus making his way along the pebbles while looking out at the fishermen faithfully practicing their trade. In one breath this first-century rabbi was inviting the fishermen to follow him, and in the next they were walking right beside him into a story that would upend their lives.

Jesus's invitation was to something as ancient as it was new. He was not inaugurating a new faith: he was fulfilling an ancient faith, but it wasn't going to purely look like either the Hellenistic culture of the Decapolis or the Jewish culture of Tiberias. It was something that transcended culture and tradition and required full immersion into a way of life that reflected the rabbi. Jesus's way countered the values of the Empire and the espoused traditions of the overly religious. In this sense, it didn't require only physically turning toward the way of Jesus, but re-orienting and re-defining truth and faithfulness. For those of the Empire, Jesus's way was confusing in the sense that he promoted selflessness and non-violence in contrast to a culture of self-promotion and violent dominance. For the religious, Jesus called into question some of the holiness codes they held most true as a means to remain faithful to the Torah and the coming Messiah.

Further, Jesus's invitation was as complex as it was simple. In this light we can see why so many didn't understand and act upon his invitation. At the same time, in his simple offers to "follow me" and "come and see," the viral invitation of this all-of-life Jewish renewal movement was under way. It was not an invitation involving only a prayer, but an invitation that would call all of life into submission to the values of the renewed kingdom.

As a people who seek to listen and submerge into the relationships of our local contexts, we hope to invite others into our homes, lives, and the way of Jesus, but we also hope to be invited into the lives of others. We follow the model of Jesus, who, after living for thirty years alongside those in the Galilee region, began to invite others toward his new way of life, but was also invited into the homes and around the tables of others. In Luke 5 Jesus is the guest of honor at the home of a former tax collector. Jesus was so embedded in deep relationships that others were willingly extending invitations to him.

SAINT PATRICK AND THE INVITATION OF THE CELTIC CHRISTIANS

There have been few historical Christian communities that have had a more significant role in shaping our rhythms of life and mission than that of Saint Patrick and the Celtic Christians. Living as a "sent" people who were committed to rhythms of common life, this band of early Christians embodied missional-monastic community in a context that was anything but conventional.

While Saint Patrick of Ireland is one of the most commonly known spiritual fathers of the past 2000 years, he is also one of the most misunderstood. Often associated with green beer, shamrocks, and the driving out of snakes, Saint Patrick's life and legacy have been greatly diminished by folklore. Because his legend is so widespread, there is rich potential for the values of the historical Saint Patrick to reach the masses if his story is retold well. Having been raised in Roman nobility and enslaved by Irish barbarians, his role as spiritual father of a hostile population was uniquely shaped by earlier parts of his life. Further, Saint Patrick's ability to create a Christian movement of engagement within a pagan Celtic spirituality offers a rich tradition that, if emulated, has the potential to ignite the hearts and imaginations of Christians around the globe.

After being kidnapped from his home in Britain as a child, Patrick spent six years in slavery tending livestock on the green hills of Ireland. During that time he had an encounter with God that forever changed the trajectory of his life and mission. While in the fields, he had a vision of his escape back to Britain. Relying on his vision, he walked 200 miles through the wilderness and boarded a ship for Britain. Roman roads often didn't extend to some of the coastal towns in Britain, so after his arrival, he and his fellow crewmates wandered the large island for twenty-eight days. Nearly starving to death, Patrick prayed for God's provision and told his captain, "Today he's going to send food right into your path—plenty to fill your bellies— because his abundance is everywhere."[2] God did provide and Patrick made it home.

The man who returned to his boyhood home was not the boy who had been kidnapped six years earlier. Patrick now had a living relationship with the God who wanted the hearts of the Romans as well as the Irish barbarians who had enslaved him. Despite being a town hero and being begged by his parents to never leave home again, Patrick had another vision in which he heard a chorus of voices saying, "Come here and walk among us."[3] So, although in very different circumstances from the first, Patrick decided to return to Ireland.

Upon Saint Patrick's arrival, the viral movement of Celtic Christian communities took shape and extended throughout the "barbarian" lands. History tells us that Patrick engaged and traveled "to the most remote parts of the island—places at the very edge of the world, places no one had ever been before."[4] He didn't go to Ireland to minister by himself, as the saint knew that the spiritual life and missionary call were not to be lived alone. In fact, the message he was working to share wouldn't have made practical sense outside of a life lived in community. The Celtic Christianity that was birthed out of Patrick didn't simply seek the transactional, individual conversion, but it invited others into a life of discipleship and practice. Monastic life set in the context of vocational mission offered a fertile foundation for a movement that was symbolized by journey rather than a static arrival of faith.

In a society that was spread thin across the island, monasticism created the first population hubs in Ireland.[5] The monastic life in Ireland wasn't as strict as many other orders in Europe as it promoted movement toward engaging the Celtic culture and reading all literature, whether Christian or pagan.[6] Unlike Roman monasteries, which were typically built in quiet, remote locations, the Celtic communities were planted right alongside the tribal settlements where the Irish people lived and worked. The prevailing opinion in the Roman church was that barbarians were not even capable of becoming Christians. They were considered illiterate, emotional, out of control. But Patrick invited these Irish barbarians into the community to taste and participate in a different way of doing life. He understood that most people need to belong before they believe. They need to be listened to and understood because when people sense that someone really understands them, they begin to believe that maybe God can understand them too.

These "barbarians" found a home through the invitation of Patrick and this new movement of Jesus followers. And it was only in the context of this invitation that they were able to step toward the invitation of God into a story that continues to be told through his community today.

RADICAL INVITATION VERSUS RADICAL HOSPITALITY

The nature of an invitation is directly influenced by the level of commitment that is inherent in the community into which one is being invited. In the relatively recent history of the church, the invitation has largely been reduced to a set of doctrinal statements or ecclesial norms. To be invited to "church" has meant attending a worship service on a Sunday morning or Wednesday night. To join a church has meant signing off on a set of stated beliefs. Further, if you don't enjoy the sermon or music, it has been normal to "try out" another church in the hopes of finding a service that better fits your personal needs for interacting with God.

I can't emphasize enough what a misguided understanding of invitation this is. It is misguided for the one who is seeking to best find something that fits his or her needs, but it is also misguided in that the churches often market themselves in a way so that the church service is the barometer for success or failure. These extractional models of church pour their time, energy, and resources into impressing those who are being invited to their community to the extent that the visitors can't help but judge the success of the church by anything other than performance. Some call this a "seeker-sensitive" church model because church leaders place an inherently higher value on creating a comfortable and excellent environment over a challenging and transparent one. Too often, churches (and the people who are part of them) following this model miss out on the opportunity to invite people into a community that strives—and often struggles—to live out the truths of Scripture in all aspects of life.

In our missional community, we seek to offer what we call radical invitations rather than radical hospitality. While our doors remain open for anyone in need of a bed or a meal (hospitality that has historical roots in most monastic orders), those who want to participate in our covenant community must accept the radical invitation of apprenticeship in the way of Jesus. Being part of a missional community is not simply attending a gathering or two each week. It is to submit all aspects of your life to Jesus and to your community of faith and to collectively practice the ways of Jesus.

Far from either a comfortable nominalist approach or a legalistic mental adherence to a doctrine, we invite people into a radical reorienting of life in the way of Jesus that is submitted to the reign of God as is manifest in his advancing kingdom. Our invitation is rooted in the breadth and depth of the invitation of God to his people. We are not simply invited into a set of propositions: we are invited into a holistic salvation that upends our values and relationships and rebuilds them in light of the person and work of Jesus. Jesus repeatedly taught us and showed us that we must lose our life to find it (see Matthew 10:39). Theologian Dietrich Bonhoeffer described Jesus's invitation with these hauntingly true words: "I bid you come and die."[7]

Such an invitation is the beginning of our journey back to God's original design and intent for humanity. He created a people designed for covenant community. We are relational beings who can't fully understand the nature of God or ourselves outside of community. Jesus, as the Messiah, was the figure who would restore the people of Israel to their true identity as a community. The Messiah wasn't viewed as one who would save individuals, but one who would restore a community to a kingdom that was submitted to God.

This radical invitation is the beginning of redemption, of the restoration God has in mind for all of his people. It is the beginning of a faith that does not remain in the minds of individuals, but is lived in the context of a community of faith. While we have far from mastered such aspirations, this is the invitation we seek to offer in our missional community.

FIELD NOTES: NIEUCOMMUNITIES VANCOUVER

Jacob's Well was the perfect place to be invited into.

Joyce, the director, was a good friend of mine from our days at Regent College, so when I moved back to Vancouver to help birth NieuCommunities in the city, we naturally reconnected. Almost immediately we both sensed that our communities could complement one another and perhaps partner in significant ways.

Jacob's Well is a faith-based community in the Downtown Eastside of Vancouver, British Columbia. It's in the poorest zip code in the whole of Canada, with the highest rate of HIV and Hepatitis C in all of North America. Needless to say, it is a place of great need.

The vision of the Jacob's Well community is to seek mutually transformative friendships with those on the margins of society and to equip others to do the same in their own contexts. They have created what might be described as a loving living room and a common table in the heart of the city to share with their friends and neighbors.

Our partnership flourished with Jacob's Well largely because their community was already living out—in visible and concrete ways—the values that we were teaching and striving to live out in our neighborhood. We were continually challenged and inspired by their warm and inviting presence among those on the margins. They invited us into their world and taught us much about God's love for all people and how to be real friends to people on the fringes rather than simply giving them food. They also taught us what it means to forge real community with people whose lives are radically different from our own.

Jacob's Well made us better people. They made us more inviting people. They taught us how to be better friends, and for that we will always be grateful.

—Amy Wilson-Roberts

FROM EXTENDING INVITATION TO RECEIVING INVITATION

The expectation of a coming Messiah who would restore Israel to the land, rebuild the Temple, and reestablish the Davidic throne was very much a Jewish one. This would be the figure, like Moses, who would deliver God's people from exile and restore the Abrahamic covenant. In this sense, it is of paramount importance to understand the arrival and work of Jesus in the context of first-century Judaism. While it was realistic for the whole world to be positively impacted by the Messiah's reestablishment of the Davidic kingdom, it was clearly "good news" first for the Jews (see Romans 2:10). If this Messiah could first restore Israel, then the whole world would have the potential of being invited into the restoration.

Although the kingdom that Jesus brought about didn't fit many of the Jewish expectations for Messianic deliverance—as is glaringly clear in Mark's description of the disciples consistently failing to understand Jesus as the Messiah—it was the early followers of the way who began to identify him as the prophesied deliverer. Jesus did restore the land, but rather than only being a small slice of land on the Mediterranean, he announced a kingdom that stretched to the ends of the earth. Jesus did rebuild the Temple, but it took the form of his resurrection and ascension to the right hand of God as king of the kingdom: Jesus *became* the Temple where people could gather to meet God. Finally, rather than overthrowing the government, Jesus's selfless sacrifice paved the way to his taking of the throne and inauguration as the permanent king of the kingdom at the right hand of God.

In short, Jesus fulfilled the Messianic requirement, but he did so in a way that ran counter to Jewish expectation. Because of this reality, Jesus's early followers took awhile to put all the pieces together to understand the nuances of Jesus's identity and the characteristics of his kingdom. It is in this light that we read Peter's encounter with the Roman soldier Cornelius in Acts 10.

Peter, as one of the leaders of this budding Jewish renewal movement that is centered on the life and work of the Messiah Jesus, is faithfully seeking to spread the good news. Although still not sure who is able to receive the good news of Jesus, this young community is growing and making itself present in homes, cities, and expanding regions surrounding the Roman Empire. They are listening to their context, submerging deeply into the fabric of society, and inviting others to join the movement.

After having a startling vision, Cornelius, the Roman army officer, finds himself seeking out Peter. Cornelius is a good guy who has shown devotion to the God of Israel and to the people around him, but he is asking the leader of this Jewish renewal movement into his home. This is a big deal for a man outside of the Jewish tradition and an even bigger deal for Peter to accept the offer to enter a Gentile home.

In the end, it was this interaction that led this young community to a deeper understanding of the vast extent of a kingdom invitation. It was not an invitation that was to be contained within the Jewish communities, but one that would transcend and transform people of all races, religions, and regions. Further, this revelation did not come about through Peter's inviting the Roman soldier into his life and faith, but by Cornelius inviting Peter into his home.

Peter and this band of believers made themselves available to the community through intentional presence and engagement. They were willing to step out of their assumed traditions and follow the Spirit's leading and receive renewed revelation that would greatly advance the kingdom of God. It is one thing to offer radical invitations to those with whom we seek relationship, but it is a whole other thing to be invited into the home, life, and story of others.

"I THOUGHT YOU'D NEVER ASK"

It was a few years ago that Christiana, one of the leaders of our community in San Diego, first ran into Darren and LaDonna. Their encounter at the local park was nothing out of the ordinary, but it was the beginning of something that would radically impact our community's life and the lives of our friends.

Along with a few other women and children in our intentional community, Christiana spends a lot of time at the local park with her two daughters. While this has proven to be one of her girls' favorite destinations, Christiana is extremely intentional with her time and interactions there: she often walks to the park in a spirit of prayer and expectation. In one of these instances, Christiana met Darren and LaDonna, who were playing at the park with their sons, for the first time. Ironically, our missional community was hosting our neighborhood Christmas party that night, and within a few hours, this young couple and their two boys were in our homes, surrounded by those who are a part of our community. Immediately intrigued by the community life and energy present, they stayed for most of the party and exchanged contact information.

After meeting with LaDonna a couple times a week at the park, Christiana invited their family over for a meal with her husband, Derek, and their two girls. It was here, in this somewhat sacred, intimate space that meeting in a private home creates, that conversation naturally led to things of faith and where Christiana and Derek explained their commitment to follow Jesus in community with a band of fellow Christians. Although Darren had been raised Jewish, he and LaDonna were fascinated by this expression of life and faith that directly impacted so many aspects of life. There was something both mysterious and compelling that they wanted more of. In fact, after spending the day helping the Rices move one afternoon, Darren pulled Christiana aside and said, "Please don't stop talking about Jesus just because I'm Jewish."

In time, Darren and LaDonna naturally became closer with other people in our intentional community. We would dress up like medieval knights for their kids' birthday parties, have them over for meals, watch football games, and babysit each other's kids. In the same way, they offered their love and hospitality to each of us in unique and authentic ways. Darren and LaDonna weren't simply growing in their relationships with separate individuals; they were growing in their relationship with a community.

We have our community worship gatherings on Sunday evenings in the living room of one of the bigger homes of one of our tribe. After a shared meal, we spend time communing with God through music, liturgy, or prayer and often have a time of teaching and conversation. These times are very intimate and offer a unifying rhythm to the life of our community. Every couple months we open these gatherings up to faith communities all over our city. They serve as a context to encourage and unify the corporate church in our city and offer a much-needed time of rest and renewal for many local pastors and leaders.

As their relationship progressed and as their mutual trust and shared life deepened, Christiana invited LaDonna to one of these city-wide worship nights. Having seen and experienced our community's commitment to Jesus take shape in other forms, there was something about this experience that brought about a deep sacredness for LaDonna. Eyes filling with tears of warmth and joy, she whispered to Christiana, "I am so honored that you would invite me into this even though I don't believe the same things you believe." Although much of what we did was foreign to LaDonna, being surrounded by people who cared so deeply for her and her family while they worshiped the God who so clearly informed the lives they were living created a space for her to feel her own connection with God.

Over time, Darren started picking up on words like *calling*, *kingdom*, and *sent people*. He was fascinated, but even more than that, he wanted to experience these realities in his own life. Although not claiming Jesus as Lord or being part of our community apprenticeship, Darren asked Derek to be his coach as he navigated the waters of living a life more in line with the divine rhythms. Opening himself up completely to this experience, Darren soon realized that his life was wrapped around making money and pursuing a life that wasn't worth living. Seeking to reorient himself around the values found in the life and teachings of Jesus, he found that he had a passion for mentoring young men and for caring deeply for those around him. With a contagious passion, Darren began to mentor a foster child in the spare time he gained from pulling back from work and spending less time traveling. His life quickly became about family, others, and the living out of a new story of what he would say was inspired by Jesus and our intentional community.

As relationships deepened and invitations were extended, Darren and LaDonna ran into an experience that shook them to the core. Somewhat unexpectedly, LaDonna's father died, and as an only child, her support network was extremely thin. The relationships that naturally took shape in a local playground quickly became the relationships that Darren and LaDonna would hold onto most tightly during this time. While Christiana and Derek offered their presence, the rest of our community brought over meals, offered childcare, and came alongside our new friends in any way possible during their time of loss.

There was no agenda to Christiana's, Derek's, or our community's love for this young family. We were simply attempting to live faithfully as participants in the missio Dei. It's not just about being a good Christian; it's as simple as being a good neighbor. In fact, it was in simply being good neighbors that we embodied the good news of Jesus.

A few months after the death of LaDonna's father, Darren sent an e-mail to our whole intentional community inviting us into their home for a celebration meal. We weren't sure exactly what that meant or how to respond. We just knew we were being invited into the home of a family for whom we all cared deeply. One by one we filed through their front doors and into a home full of warmth, laughter, and the sounds of kids having the time of their lives.

Having set up specific place mats with a personal gift for each person, Darren had us form a twenty-five-person circle in their living room. He told us, "We wanted to invite you all into our home and prepare this meal as a celebration of what you have all meant to us over the past couple years. There aren't enough words to express our gratitude to you. You are our community." Looking at a friend, our brother, most of us had a knot in our throat and tears in our eyes. I later found out that after the death in their family, Christiana and Derek had sent them a bouquet of flowers and signed the note, "From Your Community."

In the end, it wasn't the note that led Darren to describe us as his community that night; it was the invitation to shared life that has been unfolding through the everyday experiences of daily life. Further, as we stood in that circle in their living room with our glasses held high, it was no longer about our invitation to them; it was about their invitation to us. We were given the gifts of deep friendship, shared life, and communal transformation.

In a recent conversation with Darren, Christiana asked, "Would you and LaDonna be interested in getting together this next week and talking about what it could look like for you to formally join our covenant community?" Darren quickly responded, "I thought you'd never ask."

INVITATION TO THE KINGDOM BANQUET

There is a profound connection between the act of extending an invitation and the work God has in store for all creation. When we invite, we are reflecting the characteristics of God's kingdom. An invitation is the doorstep to a restoration of community. With Jesus, God's restoration project came to a culmination in the inaugurating of a kingdom that would extend to all people and all places. Whether simply inviting a friend from the local coffee shop to a neighborhood Christmas party or extending the radical invitation of Jesus apprenticeship to an aspiring leader, God's heart and plan are revealed through the inviting posture adopted by his people.

Our Integrating and Sustaining Practices

- We host a monthly picnic in our local park and invite neighbors and friends.
- We invite neighbors onto our patios and into our homes on a regular basis for shared meals and conversation.
- We invite local faith leaders to worship with us in our homes on a regular basis.
- Each year we host a neighborhood Christmas party in one of our homes.
- We strive to accept invitations from our neighbors, local businesses, and local artists to support and be present in their everyday realities.
- We invite people from all over the globe to stay with us for a time as they navigate their pilgrimage toward discernment and/or community life.

Missional Possibilities

1. What are some of the assumptions you have about what people think is actually inviting?
2. Describe an experience or a space into which you could invite someone.
3. What changes would you have to make to be more accessible and connected to the people around you?

Video Questions

1. Jon talks about the "radical invitation" that Jesus offers the disciples along the Sea of Galilee. What would a radical invitation to be a disciple look like in your unique twenty-first-century context?
2. How can you begin to get to know people in your community and make them "feel safe" without making them feel like you're simply trying to convert them?

CHAPTER 4

CONTENDING

"I want you to know how hard I am contending for you and for those at Laodicea, and for all who have not met me personally. My goal is that they may be encouraged in heart and united in love, so that they may have the full riches of complete understanding, in order that they may know the mystery of God, namely, Christ . . ." (Colossians 2:1-2).

Our world is full of issues that at times seem insurmountable. Whether we're referring to global issues such as hunger, AIDS, genocide, and war, or more local concerns such as international refugees struggling to assimilate, or single-parent families or the homeless struggling to survive, each issue and people group needs our attention. The problem is that they can be so overwhelming that we choose to simply go about our routines and ignore the areas of brokenness and injustice that surround us. However, while simply ignoring those who are in need is tempting and far too culturally acceptable, our role as God's people is to step into these stories and contend for those who are broken, hurting, and alone. We are to be the manifestation of the good news brought about with the arrival of God's kingdom.

Rebecca has become a dear friend to Jan and me as we wade through the realities of intentional community together, but she has also become a dynamic presence of invitation and advocacy in our neighborhood. In fact, Rebecca has intentionally chosen to spend less time working, which obviously has very tangible financial repercussions, so she can be available to and present in our intentional community and our neighborhood. With that vision in mind, she first started building relationships with women from the CRASH halfway home by tagging along on some of their one-day trips around San Diego County. In spending time at CRASH, Rebecca met Amber, who had been working the past seven years as a prostitute. As a result, Amber's confidence and self-esteem were in dire straits. Even though she had gone through much of her recovery program, she didn't believe she was worthy to be hired at any "normal" job and the thought of finding gainful employment brought about deep-rooted anxiety.

After meeting Amber on one of the day trips to the Del Mar Fair, Rebecca ended up connecting with her again on a morning walk with some of the CRASH women. The pained woman shared her concerns about an upcoming job interview and mentioned that she was going to have to take the bus to get there. Rebecca quickly offered to ride with her, and they proceeded to endure a three-hour bus ride to get there in time (San Diego public transit isn't exactly efficient).

It was a very hot day, and by the time they finally arrived at the interview location, Amber was sweaty and nervous. The pair rushed into the bathroom to clean up, and Rebecca looked into Amber's eyes, reminded her that Jesus was with her, and affirmed that she was more than capable to do this job well.

Amber didn't get the job, but she said that the hurdles of the entire experience would have normally brought her to a low point. Because Rebecca was with her, though, Amber was able to just laugh. More importantly, she experienced something profoundly significant in simply walking in the door for the interview that day. Her confidence was beginning to be restored and her self-esteem once again unearthed from under layers of insecurity.

Rob's wife, Laurie, took Amber to her next interview, and she got the job. This formerly broken woman has now been sober for many months, working full time, and getting to see her kids again.

Although both Rebecca and Laurie verbally affirmed Amber, their acts of contending for the renewal of her broken story spoke far more of their support and belief. Amber was no longer alone in her issues; in her newfound community, she was able to experience restoration in areas that otherwise seemed impossible.

Living in community with people like Rebecca and Laurie forces me to ask myself the questions, *Am I riding the bus with the people in my life who I have been called to love and serve? Am I willing to set aside an excessive lifestyle which can only be sustained by a certain income in order to be fully available and present to meet the needs of my community and neighborhood?*

Contending is the fourth posture of our missional apprenticeship. Having listened to the story of our context, submerged deeper into its storylines and corresponding relationships, which leads to both extending and receiving invitations, we now seek to contend for our neighbors and intentional community. In this posture, we desire to confront injustice in our city, advance the kingdom in spiritual authority, and shape people beyond our community to become everyday apprentices of Jesus.

CONTENDING AS COMMUNITY

As communities on mission, we who call ourselves followers of Jesus must contend for our neighbors. In the posture of contending, we learn to fight for God's kingdom when everything around us tells us to give up, give in, protect ourselves, and live what's comfortable. That's why I'm convinced that the very act of joining God's heart of global justice actually gives us courage to stay in the game in our own context and keep following after Jesus. When we see how much there is to fight for in the most tragic places of our world, we will be compelled to contend for God's kingdom reign in our own lives and families and communities and neighborhoods.

While elements of social contending take myriad forms, listed below are some of the ways our communities contend for those who live in our neighborhoods:

Contending for the Poor and Displaced

- Rob works with local refugees who are seeking to start their own business by facilitating a microloan program.
- Matt advocates for local Eritreans as they seek sustainable employment.
- Laurie, Maria, Janny, and Carli come alongside refugees each week to help them integrate into a new culture by teaching them English and hosting activities for their children.
- Jon and Sophia offer employment to local artists in San Diego and Tijuana by selling their art at Make Good.

Contending for Creation

- Rebecca's husband, Chaz, and I manage the Golden Hill Farmers' Market as a way to support local food movements, farmers, and businesses.
- Rebecca and Chaz host a local food cooperative that gives people in our neighborhood access to ethically-grown beef and dairy products.
- Colin has given much of his life to bridging the gap between the church and ecology by creating a permaculture network of missional communities.[1]

Contending for the Kingdom in Spiritual Authority

- Through learning the story of our city, we seek to contend against the powers of darkness that exist by interceding as God's sent ones in spiritual authority.
- We engage the depths of the neighborhood in order to contend for its freedom from spiritual and social bondage through prayer and advocacy.

Our sister communities in Vancouver, Canada, and Pretoria, South Africa contend for their local contexts through a variety of avenues unique to the stories and issues of their cities.

- Members of our Vancouver community have intentionally taken jobs at coffee shops in the poorest parts of the city as a way to bring life to spaces often forgotten.
- As a community, they have been active participants in social protests and marches for fair wages.
- They have spoken out against the recent Olympics, which turned buildings into hotels rather than affordable housing for residents.
- In South Africa, our community is active in being a presence of reconciliation between segregated white and black communities who still carry with them the heavy weight of apartheid.
- They have studied the history of the region and come alongside those who are living in oppressive conditions in townships.

CONTENDING FOR COMMUNITY

It is clear that we need to contend for justice, our neighborhood, and the already-not-yet realities of the kingdom, but we must also contend for our intentional communities before and while simultaneously contending for our context. I have talked with a number of people whose intentional communities never made it to their first anniversary though they started with great intentions and inspirational ideals. In many cases, the problem was that they didn't first learn how to contend for their community.

In some senses, intentional community has become trendy and overly idealized, which has created a false impression that community life is somehow easy. The reality is that living in covenant community is difficult. It requires a humility and willingness to shed some unnecessary ideals for the sake of the good movement of the community. We do no one any favors by ignoring these realities of community life.

In short, if we don't expose some of the myths of our own community, we really have no chance to contend for our context. We can't have one without the other. There is plenty to talk about in regard to contending for justice in our cities and against dark and opposing forces we regularly encounter, but for the rest of this chapter, let's shift our focus to contending for community. Our hope is to highlight and equip communities to make it for the long haul.

GOD'S PEOPLE: A COVENANT COMMUNITY

The idea of living as a covenant community is not a new concept. In fact, in the story of God, it is clear that covenant community has always been God's ideal organization of his people as well as the type of community that God put in place as a means to be good news to the rest of the world.

Although a covenant is a two-way contract, the covenant between Yahweh and Noah offered no room for human response or amendment (see Genesis 9). The Abrahamic covenant didn't have specific expectations or requirements outside of male circumcision and a holistic, faithful walk with God (see Genesis 15 and 17). The covenant that was established through Moses between God and the people of Israel was much more extensive although it was not forced upon God's people: "'We will do everything the LORD has said'" (Exodus 19:8). It was a mutual agreement to commit to a specific way of life. The contract was not approached as two parties entering arbitration: it was an interaction that was rooted in the belief that this commitment would be beneficial to the parties involved as well as to the surrounding community. Rather than being self-seeking, it sought the good of the other.

This covenant was not simply with Moses, but with the budding community which was to be a reflection of God's love for humanity. It functioned as the framework for the type of community they were agreeing to be—in work, with family, in worship, in service, and so on, and was an all-of-life commitment that was worth submitting to out of the hopes for what was to come, both in the present and in the future.

A few themes are important to note in understanding the nature of the covenant established between God and his people—identity, invitation, and vocation.

FIELD NOTES: NIEUCOMMUNITIES SOUTH AFRICA

Every year around the middle of July, I (Bryan) would begin to have an internal struggle. For NieuCommunities South Africa, July marked the beginning of our practicing of the contending posture, which tended to be one of our more challenging postures as well as one of the most rewarding. It was during our practice of this posture that we addressed matters such as interpersonal relationships, injustice, and the needs of those who lived around us. It was also the posture where we challenged our everyday way of life and how that lined up with our values. One of the ways that we addressed this was through the spiritual practice of simplicity in relation to our time, relationships, and money.

One of the specific ways that our community practiced simplicity was by trying to live off half of our discretionary income for the month of August. This included all the money that we normally spent on things like food, entertainment, gas, and household products. We would then collect the leftover money at the end of the month and use it to care for others who were in need.

For our family, this was one of the most eye-opening months of our year. Could I plan my day so I could make fewer trips, use less gas, and waste less time? What foods were inexpensive, yet nutritious and filling? What were alternative ways our family could spend time together that didn't require money or travel? Were our values truly shaping our lives? Although we usually began this month with some moans and groans, many of us came to hold this process, and its affect on our lives, as dear and necessary.

—Bryan and Daleen Ward

IDENTITY

This community was set apart. It was unique to Yahweh, the God of Israel. Not only had this God brought the community out of exile in Egypt; he had provided for their daily physical needs. God chose this people to be a physical representation to the rest of the nations of God's saving work and daily provision (see Exodus 19:4-8). He chose them to embody his characteristics of love and invitation so that a world gone bad might turn back to the creator who made everything good.

This community was marked in very tangible ways. First, their identity was shaped around the work of Yahweh in earlier parts of their story, namely in their delivery from Egypt. Second, the building of the tabernacle carried the very presence of Yahweh: the God and creator of the cosmos was accessible and open to meeting with his covenant community in very real ways. Finally, it was marked with the mandate to represent Yahweh to the rest of the world with the hope of restoring humanity to the one true God. It was a community shaped around a covenant with Yahweh and with each other, while at the same time being a community on mission for the good of the nations. The challenge for Moses and this young community was being faithful, both to each other and to Yahweh. Their story was a story of contending for a community that had to remain faithful to God and each other for the sake of all humanity.

INVITATION

The invitation of a covenant community is exceedingly different from that of a community without such an identity. A covenant community can invite others to join as they are, but not without the expectation that the invited will take on the identity of the rest of the community as is made clear in their covenant. This was the reality of the people of Israel. Central to the covenant that was agreed upon by God and Israel (as is made clear in the Torah), this community was to be a place of restoration and welcome for the alien, the foreigner, the poor, and the widowed (see Leviticus 19:34). Others outside of the covenant community could find a new home, but not without the expectation that they would take on the covenant of the rest of the community. They had to begin to dance in the rhythms of the story God was telling among his people.

At this point in Israel's story, the Passover was the celebration of their most significant chapter, when Yahweh miraculously delivered them from the exile and violence of the Egyptian Pharaoh. To celebrate Passover was not simply to celebrate an earlier chapter in the story: it was to acknowledge that story as their own story. Foreigners who fully submitted themselves to the covenant and re-oriented their identity with that of the community were able to take part in this sacred celebration (see Exodus 12:48).[2] In short, the radical invitation was extended but held those who accepted it to the same responsibilities and corresponding consequences for failed responsibility.

In this sense, an invitation to covenant community is drastically different from the invitation of most churches. Israel was as welcoming as possible without compromising the unique identity of their people as was marked by their agreement with Yahweh to be a people on mission for the good of the world. They were inviting people not to a gathering or event, but into a way of life with a new identity shaped by earlier parts of their story and by the aspirations of a new future for the whole cosmos.

> So members of other ethnic groups are free to join Yahweh's people. From the beginning Israel lives with permeable boundaries. The boundaries are important; if Israel becomes indistinguishable from other peoples, God's purpose through Abraham cannot be fulfilled. Yet the permeability is also important, and for the same reason.[3]

VOCATION

Having entered into covenant community with God and each other, the people of God were to remain faithful to their word by obeying the commands given to them at Sinai. By holding fast to their God and their covenant, it was this community that God commissioned to be good news to the rest of the world and point people back to the restorative love of God. In a pluralistic world that worshiped many different gods and idols, Israel was to submit to the one true God, Yahweh. Further, by remembering the delivering role Yahweh had played in earlier parts of their story, this community was to be marked not by power and prestige, but by faithful submission to the God who was faithful and present. It was to be an alternative community that reflected the good news by living radically different from the world around them yet remaining radically engaged and inviting.

EXILE AND RESTORATION

The rest of the story is marked by Israel's obedience (or disobedience) in living as a covenant community. As a young community learning the way of Yahweh, they sought to contend for community, and there were very tangible results when they did it well or when they did it poorly. Their story is one of exile and restoration. Yet, the other party in their covenant, Yahweh, continued to pursue them and offer restoration back into the family of God. The punishment was exile, a distinct break from community, while restoration took the form of community, both with God and his people.

The story of Israel tells us a lot of things, but two things stand out for the sake of this conversation. First, God calls his people to be in covenant relationship with him. Living in covenant community had very specific implications for the way life would be organized for Israel. This was the model for community life that God chose in order for his people to remain faithful to him and be a conduit of his restoration project to the rest of humanity.

Second, living in covenant community is not easy. Time and time again, the people of God failed to live faithfully, and as a result, their intimacy with God and with each other broke down. Worse, their ability to be good news to the rest of the world was compromised and God's plan delayed. Often we find them saying, "Yes, I'm in. This will be easy!" (see Exodus 19:8), but a short time later they are building idols and seeking a leadership structure that runs in direct opposition to their covenant (worshiping a golden calf and seeking a king). While God always remained faithful to contend for them, the people had to contend time and time and again to remain on mission.

"My relationship with God always, and must ever be, about how I am participating in the narrative of God's people."[4]

God chose to enter into relationship with a group of people who were far from perfect. In the same way, we who are far from perfect enter into relationships with other people who are far from perfect. What happens when you put together a group of imperfect people who share the same covenant, but who also bring along their baggage, expectations, and contrasting personalities? You get a covenant community. You get us. There are some great things that have come out of our life and ministry, but there are also many painful experiences that have made us all question whether living in community is really worth it.

It is costly, and we must contend for the life we know God has called us to faithfully live. Like the community of Israel, we are marked by our identity, grow deeper through our radical invitation to Jesus apprenticeship, and extend through our vocation of mission.

EXPOSING THE MYTHS AND REALITIES OF COMMUNITY

God created men and women as communal creatures. In addition to being ontologically designed to be in union with the Creator, we were designed to be in communion with fellow humans and to the rest of the created order. But, as we can see in the community of Israel and all around us in our web of relationships, living in covenant community is not easy.

Humans are ontologically wired for community. While no one would deny that living in community is difficult, practitioners of the missional church have been vastly under-resourced in regard to overcoming the myths of community. It is often perceived that community will come naturally if a group of like-minded individuals come together with the same vision of life and faith. This may be true for some, but the rest of us are going to have to fight, claw, and intentionally contend for the life of our communities if we are going to make it for the long haul.

I joined NieuCommunities with some of this blind idealism. Having read all the books that told the dynamic and compelling stories of communities living on mission, I couldn't wait to jump into the relationships that I subconsciously assumed would cure all of the relational pain and discontentment I had experienced in previous forms of faith community. I had finally found "it," and I assumed that of course everyone would not only leave room for my ideals to be made into reality, but they would also actually have the same ideals as me. Right?

TOWARD COMMUNITY

In his classic work *The Different Drum: Community Making and Peace*, M. Scott Peck identifies four stages that everyone passes through in the creation of genuine community, where every member:

1. is known and knows others;
2. is loved and loves others;
3. is served and serves others.[5]

Our community has added an additional stage before Peck's beginning point. So, here are the five stages that we believe all relationships must pass through on the road to satisfying, enjoyable, sustainable community.

Stage 1: Casual

This first stage is the "acquaintance," surface level. Every culture has a level of polite, even friendly interactions that no one pretends is intimate or genuine community. It's a natural level of relationship that is legitimate and usually necessary.

Stage 2: Pseudo-Community

Pseudo-community is a legitimate form of community but a shallow one—and just a shadow of what it could be.

- All acquaintances moving from casual community toward deeper community will pass through pseudo-community.
- It's the "honeymoon" phase of community.
- We put our best foot forward and our best face on. We're well- well-behaved and polite.
- We often speak in generalities and clichés, and we tend to agree with everyone.
- We hide our differences from each other, hoping no one will notice.
- We ignore infractions—whether small or great—no matter how much they bother us.
- We stuff offenses down because we don't want to make waves or cause trouble. At least not yet.

The difference between casual relationships and pseudo-community is that in causal relationships, we don't pretend we're in community. In fact, we wouldn't even use that word. But we begin to slide into pseudo-community when we start to think that this friendship, this group, is true community. We start using the word "community" or at least start acting like we're experiencing it.

Stage 3: Chaos

It's easy enough to maintain pseudo-community when we see each other for only an hour or two each week. But when we're doing life together, it won't be long before all those annoyances and grievances we've been ignoring spill out!

Although a necessary step in the process toward community, there are a couple communication problems that often don't allow aspiring communities to navigate through a time of chaos. First, many of us don't know how to tell the truth when we need to. Second, we often don't know how to hear the truth! Chaos is threatening and often painful. It doesn't feel good. We don't want to stay there. So what do we do? We almost always resort to one of two options:

> Option 1: Revert back to pseudo-community
> It was easier before. Let's just go back to the way it was. We start hearing things like, "Why can't we just get along? I want things to be the way they were."
>
> Option 2: Retreat from the relationship
> We just bail altogether. We start saying things like, "It shouldn't be this hard." "I don't need this." "I thought I could do life with these people, but maybe I can't." Sometimes the withdrawal is physical—other times it's emotional. It is here that most of the aspiring communities I have interacted with lose traction and throw in the towel.[6]

But the only way to truly experience deep, satisfying community and deep personal transformation is to move beyond chaos to (and through) catharsis.

Stage 4: Catharsis

This stage is a deeper form of community. Catharsis literally means coming clean or emptying oneself. We must empty ourselves of all the obstacles to community that are in us if we want to experience community. We do that by confessing our shortcomings to one another and to God, by taking responsibility for our own emotions and happiness, and by suspending judgment of others while we tend to the dark places in our own hearts.

Stage 5: Deeper Community

We reach this stage when we are 1) truly known and know others; 2) loved and love others; 3) served and serve others. There's no faking or feigning because deeper community happens when relationships are real and transforming. Deeper community is what we experience when we have relentless friends who:

- accept us as we are, but who love us too much to allow us to remain this way.
- are committed to a complete transformation of our character.

When we've found friends like that, we've found real community.

MYTHS OF COMMUNITY

Keeping in mind the path and process of the pilgrimage toward community as previously outlined, we have unearthed six myths of community (of the many that exist!) over the past decade of navigating and helping others navigate the sometimes-tumultuous waters of intentional community. Before moving forward, it is important to note that I adamantly believe the effort required to develop true community is well worth it. In exposing these myths,

I hope to better equip you and your community as you enter the life-giving realities of covenant community. Like marriage or life-long friendship, the relational dynamics of community life require healthy expectations in order to avoid debilitating disappointment.

Myth #1: Perfect Harmony

This myth says that we'll all get along really easily and naturally with little to no conflict. After all, we all showed up here, so we must all be on the same page, right? This myth means that we assume that we will all be naturally interested in each other's lives and we'll discover things about each other with which we strongly connect. We also assume that we're in similar places in our maturity, experience, and readiness, and since we're all equally committed to the same things, we'll all be willing to make similar sacrifices.

However, the reality is we're not all at the same place, and we may never be. That's okay, though. There will always be some dissonance in a community. Dissonance doesn't mean you don't have community; in fact, it might actually mean you do! Or, as we saw in the stages of community, you're at least on your way there.

Myth #2: Absolute Agreement

This myth does not refer to harmony in relationships, but to harmony in decisions and direction. It is the myth that we'll always agree or arrive at a consensus because that's what happens in community. This myth is the naive belief that no one will ever have to yield their opinion to the group because we'll always end up on the same page if we just talk long enough. It is the belief that if we're yielding enough to each other and to the Spirit we will never have to agree to disagree.

There's another assumption in this myth that's a little more subtle but pretty significant: it's the assumption that we won't need distinct roles or responsibilities because we're a community and everybody will decide on everything together, and we won't move until we do. When we do that, we flirt with a denial of the gifts and roles with which God has gifted his church. The reality is, there will always be disagreements and differences in perspectives. There will be differences in gifts and responsibilities. In our communities, we've found that the answer isn't agreeing on everything; it's finding a way to go forward even when we don't agree.

Myth #3: Raw Pleasure

This is the myth that being honest, raw, or authentic means we have the right to say whatever we're feeling whenever we want and thinking that people will actually appreciate that. This myth leads to thinking that unbounded authenticity is always good and welcomed. In fact, it is thinking that unbounded authenticity *is* community. Further, the myth of raw pleasure is the belief that now that we are in community, the door is wide open for us to say whatever we're feeling whenever we're feeling it—because healthy community requires complete honesty 100 percent of the time. It's concluding that messiness and confusion are the reality of community life and that people actually prefer messiness over harmony, peace, and light-hearted adventure.

The reality is that community is not—and never has been—a green light to be mean or insensitive. Chaos is not synonymous with community. In healthy communities, love and kindness will always trump raw, self-serving disclosure.

Myth #4: Truth At All Costs

While raw pleasure is more about personal disclosure, this myth is more about the idea of speaking "truth" to others. This is the myth that in community, we have a duty to point out people's faults as soon as we see them. It is the assumption that we need to deliver the truth that we know as soon as we know it. It's the belief that people want and need to hear truth more than they want and need to feel loved. This myth assumes that we can freely share our convictions and opinions at just about any time because being in community gives us a green light to address people's "ignorance" or their personal issues at any time.

But, the reality is there is still a right time and a right way to share convictions and people will always have different convictions . . . and you may even be wrong!

Myth #5: It's All Fixable

This myth is the common assumption that communities are miracle workers—that if a need is shared in community, the community must have the ability to fix it. Those who hold this belief often assume that if we need help beyond our community, we're not a "true" community. Believing this myth also leads us to jump to the conclusion that people share things openly because they want us to fix their problems. Maybe they do, but maybe they just need us to listen and empathize with them.

The reality is that we're human and we won't be able to meet everyone's needs. There are many great resources outside of our community (pastors, counselors, spiritual directors, coaches, and so on) that we would be foolish and arrogant not to access.

Myth #6: True Community Is Always Communal

When people visit our community, they are often surprised that we don't all live in one house. The assumption seems to be that true community requires a common roof. Many communities have chosen that form, and it has worked well for them. It certainly brings people together, and we agree that proximity is vital to organic community. There are also obvious environmental and economic benefits to shared living that should not be discounted. However, there are downsides to communal life as well: the biggest negative is probably the time and energy that are required to maintain peace and order in communal space. Sharing space is *not* the same thing as sharing life.

We have opted for a slightly different approach while still valuing proximity and a sense of shared space. We made the decision to live close to one another (all within a ten-minute walk) and to inhabit the same neighborhood rather than the same house. Some of us do share houses with each other, some of us live in separate apartments in the same building, and some of us live in our own homes. We share our lives, we share our neighborhood, and we share a common covenant to do life in a particular way. For us, making these choices has created real community.

FELLOWSHIP OF THE MAT

In Mark 2 we find Jesus in Capernaum, surrounded by masses of interested people. Verse two says, "They gathered in such large numbers that there was no room left, not even outside the door." The house was full. There was no way anyone else was going to gain access to this miracle-working rabbi. But then the clay and straw started falling down all around them. There was something going on on the roof and as everyone looked up, a hole appeared and a paralyzed man descended before Jesus. Jesus then forgave this man of his sins, healed him of his paralysis, and sent him on his way.

All of this happened when there was "no more room left." The man was broken, but then his community picked up his mat. These four men weren't going to allow their friend to be broken any longer. They chose to contend for his well-being and bring him to the place of restoration.

Shaun committed to our community a few years ago after having spent the majority of his life in Mexico on mission among the native population. He is one of the most relational and pastoral individuals I have ever met, and each time I step away from spending time with this dear friend, I feel heard, loved, and encouraged. In many ways, he is used as a "healer" in the lives of broken individuals and communities.

Recently, Shaun was enduring an extended season of depression and emotional pain. His brokenness led him to withdraw from community life and into himself. It was at this time that our intentional community chose to circle his mat and contend for his healing. Through extended times of prayer, listening, and presence, our community brought him to the feet of Jesus. It was hard, slow, and at times uncomfortable, but it is the call of covenant community. In the end, we all need the restoration and healing found in Jesus, but without a community to carry us to his feet, it is easy to believe the lie that there is "no more room."

For a community to carry someone to Jesus, the one being carried must be willing to acknowledge his or her brokenness. I wonder if the paralytic in Mark 2 looked at his friends like they were crazy when they asked him if they could carry him to the healing rabbi. I can imagine that he considered the idea, then nodded his head, allowing them to lift his body onto the mat. Similarly, our friend Shaun had to intentionally invite us into his pain in order for us to contend for his well-being.

At least a few things happen when we acknowledge our brokenness and need for healing with the help of our community.

- We recognize we need Jesus. We need his touch, his presence, his healing, and his forgiveness. Much like the paralytic was healed when he was taken to Jesus, that's where we become whole.
- We realize how much we need each other. We need each other to carry us to Jesus because we can't always get there on our own.
- We experience deep community and communion with God. Dietrich Bonhoeffer said it like this:

  > A man who confesses his sins in the presence of a brother knows that he is no longer alone with himself; he experiences the presence of God in the reality of the other person. As long as I am by myself in the confession of my sins everything remains in the dark, but in the presence of a brother the sin has to be brought into the light.[7]

Further, when we begin to view our communities as ones that will contend for each other by picking up one another's mats, we become a fellowship of the mat.

- We become an honest community. We act as wounded healers, not heroes. Sometimes we carry others; sometimes we need to be carried.
- We become other-centered. We live knowing that community is not all about us or having our own needs and expec-

tations met. It's about helping others get to Jesus. Most of us probably don't think that that kind of self-absorption or sense of entitlement is still in us, but it runs deeper than we'd like to admit.

We become missional. Our other-centeredness takes us beyond this community. Jean Vanier wrote,

> A community is never there just for itself or for its own glory. It comes from and belongs to something much greater and deeper: the heart of God to bring humanity to fulfillment. A community is never an end in itself; it is but a sign pointing further and deeper, calling people to love.[8]

- As a community, we continually struggle against the Western tendency to pursue autonomous lives. Rather than independence, we feel called to interdependence not just as individuals but as families. Whether we're caring for each other's children so we can avoid day care costs or we're opening our homes to individuals to "join" our family by moving into guest bedrooms, we don't seek to navigate the path to the feet of Jesus alone. Having experienced the sacred realities of intentional community, we wouldn't want to.

YIELDING IDEALS FOR KINGDOM GOOD

Before I stepped into covenant community, I had built a fantasyland of "intentional community" which assumed that everyone would want to share meals everyday, raise chickens in the backyard, use paper rather than plastic, pray together three times a day, and vacation together. I thought that's what living in intentional community looked like. But over the years I've learned that if I am going to experience covenant community and submit myself to the work God is doing in a group of people, my personal ideals can't become a stumbling block in the road along which our community is moving.

It wasn't until I shed some of my personal ideals that I was fully able to contend for my community and the ideals we had established as a cohesive unit. It is acceptable, even necessary, that we don't all share the same ideals. Being part of a community requires that we communicate honestly, openly, and respectfully. When we lay everything out, we can prayerfully sift through it all together and build a way forward that leads us all toward each other, our neighbors, and most importantly, God.

If we are to be missional communities, we must contend for areas of injustice in our neighborhoods, but in order to do this for the long haul we must first embrace the difficult road to community, expose commonly held myths, and learn to carry each other's mats to the feet of Jesus.

Our Integrating and Sustaining Practices

Contending for Our Neighborhood

- It begins with understanding our local injustices. We attend and participate in forums, discussions, protests, community planning committees, and so on to add our voice and our name into the dialogue.
- We serve and volunteer in places where marginalized people of our society go for help and restoration.
- We consciously hang out in places, eat in places, take our kids into places where our society tells us it's not okay to do

so. We do this with wisdom and courage, knowing that the ways of Jesus cross over every societal barrier.

- We revitalize the soil and plant urban gardens and invite our neighbors to share our plots.
- We walk deeply with our friends and neighbors who are hurting and we invite our community to surround them with a communal love that often is received with a sense of gratitude.
- We regularly take prayer walks through our neighborhood to pray against darkness and to invite the light of Christ to permeate our neighborhood.
- We attempt to understand the spiritual dynamics of our city and seek to disarm supernatural opposition and oppression.

Contending for Community

- We take personality and temperament tests and inventories to better understand ourselves and those with whom we're in community.
- We practice regular times of corporate confession.
- We covenant to honor each other's names.
- We gently call each other out when one of us falls into a style of communication that tears down rather than builds up.
- We allow for questions, differences, doubt, diversity, and even disagreements. We remind each other that what holds us together is the mission of God, *not* the strength of our friendships or how we agree on every point of controversy in Scripture.
- We practice healing prayer for the body and soul.

Missional Possibilities

1. What issues of injustice do you and your faith community face in your context and how might God be nudging you to contend for them?
2. Participating in a covenant community can be extremely difficult. Oftentimes, people make an unconscious choice to give up rather than make a conscious decision to contend for deep community. What is your experience with this? Have you made it past the "tunnel of chaos?"
3. Oftentimes, we are called to "contend" for each other by carrying each other to Jesus. Who has God burdened you to carry, and how can you tangibly live that out this week?

Video Questions

1. On the video, Jon says, "If we don't contend for the good of our community, to learn how to wade through conflict, to learn how to hold each other's ideals in tension and to begin to pave a way forward that is rooted in the mission of God, we aren't going to be able to contend for anyone." Where in your life are you wasting effort in conflict? How could you better use that energy to contend for those in your community?
2. Why do you think Christians sometimes fail to "speak well of each other" or to come alongside those who need us to contend for them and "bring dignity to their lives?"

CHAPTER 5

IMAGINING

"The imagination is our way into the divine imagination, permitting us to see wholly—as whole and holy—what we perceive as scattered, as order what we perceive as random."[1]

About a year after we moved from Northern California down to San Diego to join the NieuCommunities tribe in Golden Hill, Jan and I made a trip back up north to share about the life and ministry to which we had willingly given our lives. As I shared our core values of communion with God, community with others, and deep engagement in our context, I could see that most of those in the room were tracking with me. Diving deeper, I elaborated on the ways such values are fleshed out through life in intentional covenant community and living on mission in the places on the margins of society. It was here that our paradigm for life and mission began to greatly differ from that of most people in the room.

Rather than meeting in a church building, we meet in our living rooms.

Rather than living private lives miles from each other, we all live within a ten-minute walk from each other, and many share living spaces permanently.

Rather than having outreach programs to bring people to our services, we intentionally build relationships that force us to extend out of our comfort zones and into the everyday realities of others.

Rather than trying to live on more, we seek to live on less.

Rather than filling staff roles out of necessity, we seek to create a context in which people serve out of their God-given gifts, which organically forms the life and function of our faith community.

It's not that those in the room were doing anything wrong; it's simply that we were doing something outside the paradigm of the majority of modern American faith communities. While some had little or nothing to offer to our conversation, I saw a dear friend of my parents standing in the back of the room with tears welling up in his eyes. Before I could say a word, he looked at me and said, "I want to be part of that kind of church community. That seems like life the way God intended it."

Something that far transcended the paradigm he had lived in for so long had captured this man's imagination. In fact, it took something radically different from what he had known in order for this divine imagination to captivate his thinking and vision for life and faith. He hadn't been exposed or freed to imagine life outside of the way things were, and when he finally identified something God had revealed to him, he was moved in profound ways.

As Wendell Berry so beautifully articulates in the quote at the beginning of this chapter, the divine imagination gives us the ability to see what formerly seemed so "different" or "random" as ordered and whole. The divine imagination pulls us out of our complacent numbness that often captures us within paradigms that have become too comfortable and allows us to see what God may be doing far beyond our view. Divine imagination transcends the constructs that swallow us and frees us to live into a new story that is marked by kingdom anticipation, advancement, and hope. It shakes us from a posture of maintenance for the sake of adopting a posture that will set us free to live in the way God designed his creation to thrive and support his restoration project.

The imagining posture is not one of fairy tales and science fiction. There are no glass slippers or alternate realities. The divine imagination allows us to see things as they really are—to engage reality in the way Jesus desired when he announced a new kingdom and a new way of life. Embracing God's imagination for us and our communities connects to our longings in very practical ways. Whereas idealism often remains disconnected and disembodied from reality, living out of our divine imagination is living out the reality of the kingdom in the here and now. It is taking on the eyes through which we were created to see all along. Some may call this discerning and living out God's will for your individual and communal lives.

In this posture, we desire to discern God's call on our lives, to live into our role as co-creators, and to see in our mind's eye the kind of transformational faith community God wants us to pursue. As a missional-monastic community whose members are seeking to develop leaders and neighborhoods in the countercultural way of Jesus, we desire to foster the reception of God's imagination for his people. Further, we seek to be a community of practice that allows God's imagination to inform our lives by faithfully treading the path of experimentation and implementation in tangible ways. Finally, by opening ourselves to the divine imagination, we are at the same time committing to be sent wherever and to whomever God sends us.

JOINING THE STORY

From the beginning of the scriptural story, we encounter a God who is consistently seeking out his people as a way to draw them back into the community for which they were designed. God seeks to be in intimate relationship with humanity; he desires for humans to live in intimate community with one another, and the whole created order is designed to function in a rhythm of communal interdependence.

Early in the story of humanity, God's people break community with him, which leads to broken relationships with one another and the cosmos. They are often able to see only what is right in front of them, and it becomes the norm for humanity to make decisions that serve themselves rather than the interdependent created order established by God.

In Genesis 12 we find God seeking out humanity as a way to offer them a lifeboat back to community with himself, each other, and the cosmos. The restoration project is under way. Yahweh interacts with Abram (who would become the patriarch of the community of Israel) by telling him, "'Go from your country, your people and your father's household to the land I will show you'" (12:1).

Abram, who is living a seemingly normal life, gets a word from Yahweh that transcends his understanding of reality and his vision for the future. Little does he know that this call will change the course of his life as well as the life of the community of God for all time. God desires to restore what is broken and calls on Abram to be the leading character in the drama for which Abram hasn't even been given the script.

Abram accepts the call and begins to step into the divine imagination God has for his people. The drama is under way, but in order to be an active participant in the story, Abram has to be in tune and act upon the divine imagination given by God, which transcends what would have been reality for the patriarch. Abram goes to this land, the place where the people of God would be restored. Although the land is occupied (see Genesis 12:6-7), Abram sees that Yahweh is at work.

Then comes Moses.

At this point in the story, Yahweh is still pursuing the restoration of his people, a people who now find themselves oppressed. When in exile, present hope is hard to find—having an imagination for a redeemed and restored future is almost impossible. It is in this time and place that Yahweh turns to a Hebrew man who happened to grow up among the Empire's nobility, but now finds himself pursuing a life of anonymity in the fields of Midian.

Exodus 3:1 to 4:14 tells an extended drama of Yahweh doing everything he can to spark the imagination within Moses for his good as well as for the good of God's people and God's plan to restore his creation. Each time Yahweh proves himself worthy to be followed and obeyed, Moses seems to come up with an excuse to remain in anonymity among the people of God. But Yahweh is persistent. There are sticks turned to snakes, a fiery, talking bush, and leprosy both given and healed. Finally, Yahweh offers Aaron as a partner in this saving program of the people of God.

God desires to set things right, to make whole what has been broken. He needs his people to have the eyes to see past what is right in front of us and step into the master plan that is unfolding despite our hesitation to partner with him. God has dreams for each of us (both individually and communally); we must only step faithfully into them. We need communities that create contexts that foster such imagination.

Once Moses opens himself up to the divine imagination God has for him and his people, he becomes the leader he was created to be all along. He is the Messianic deliverer who brings a people in need into a covenant community with God. Further, it is the provision Yahweh shows through the faithfulness of Moses that forever marks the people of God as ones who are not forgotten, but who are delivered by the God who is in the process of making all things right.

It's important to note that Moses' faithfulness as one who would discern God's divine imagination for him as well as allow that imagination to inform and enflesh itself through action doesn't remain unique to him. This countercultural imagination takes root in his community, the people of Israel. Although at times they fail in their prophetic vocation, they become a people who are marked by a different way of life and value system. In short, they create a context in which living out their divine imagination isn't rare: it is normative.

The God who pursues humanity through Abram (later known as Abraham) and Moses continues to pursue his people with the hope of restoring his people through the person of Jesus. Jesus arrives proclaiming the kingdom of God as the reign of God being made manifest on earth. Further, he tells his followers to seek first his kingdom (see Matthew 6:33). It is no longer only about waiting for an expected deliverer in the future; it is about entering the kingdom life and restoration in Jesus in the here and now. This is a drastic re-imagining of what life can and shall be for the people of God. It is a new paradigm that requires God's people to once again submit themselves to the divine imagination God has for them.

If life were a compass, the kingdom of God would be "true north." This is life as it was meant to be. And not just for the sake of individually being aligned with the heart of God, but for the sake of being an active participant in the advancement of the kingdom. The kingdom that Jesus proclaimed through word and deed did not meet the expectations of the kingdom God's people were waiting for. This kingdom was a whole new paradigm for life and faith. As such, like Yahweh working miraculously through a burning bush to ignite Moses' divine imagination, God miraculously interacted with his followers to ignite and reform their imagination.

Whether evidenced in Peter seeing visions while praying on a rooftop (see Acts 10:9-16) or Paul being blinded on the road to Damascus (see Acts 9), God does not allow his people to lose sight of his ultimate goal of restoring his people to community with him, each other, and the whole created order. It is in these "conversion" moments that God breaks through what we have always known and invites us into a new way of living and thinking. He offers us an imagination that directly informs our actions. And, when God's people are open to the divine imagination, the things that we formerly thought could never happen become reality.

NAVIGATING TRUE NORTH

About five years ago, I first had the (admittedly rather morbid) vision of myself on my deathbed as an old man and of someone asking me, "So did you really live life to the full as God created you to do?" In this vision, I stumbled over my words for a second and then humbly looked up and replied, "No, I didn't."

Soon after this realization, I began to evaluate all aspects of my life. What was it that was bringing life to my community and me? Conversely, what was debilitating me or keeping me from fully stepping into my vocation as an apprentice of Jesus? For me it was a variety of things that included a constant need to meet others' expectations, complacency as a result of an incomplete understanding of the role of the church, and an overall acceptance of the myth of the ever-elusive American Dream.

While each of these contributed to my life lacking a holistic expression of Jesus followership, the root issue was a lack of understanding of the kingdom of God and my specific role in the community that has been commissioned to advance it. I had become content with a life that was less than what God desires for his people and as a result failed to have eyes to see the divine imagination God had for me.

In our missional community, we seek to tap into God's divine imagination for our community by navigating toward true north while discerning how each of us uniquely contributes to this communal movement. Each of has a unique place to which God wants to take us—a unique direction, a specific point on the compass—and the diversity of our journeys is beautiful. But we all have one thing in common: we all need to orient everything off the same fixed point—true north.

LIFE AS IT WAS MEANT TO BE LIVED

In the Sermon on the Mount, Jesus tells his followers, "'Seek first his kingdom and his righteousness, and all these things will be given to you as well'" (Matthew 6:33). Above all else, Jesus says, "Pursue my kingdom." But what is the kingdom of God? It's the life we've been invited to live, the life we were created to live. Dallas Willard, a theologian and philosopher, defined the kingdom of God as life as it was meant to be lived in all its wonder, life as God intended it to be experienced, and the place where what God wants to happen actually happens and where God's ways are lived and experienced.[2] That's our true north. That's what we measure everything against and what we use to align everything in our lives.

You might be wondering why true north isn't simply Jesus. Well, Jesus is certainly within the kingdom because every kingdom has a king, and when Jesus asks us to seek the kingdom of God, he is asking us to make him our king. But embracing the kingdom is more than just embracing a relationship with Jesus; it's bigger than that. It's also an invitation to partner with Jesus in bringing heaven to earth and helping others experience life as it was meant to be lived.

So what would that life look like? When you think about life as God intended it, you might think of biblical images like lions lying down with lambs or a banquet where "the least" enjoy a feast. But Jesus also said that the kingdom of God is near—it's for right here, right now as well as for eternity.

When you think about what the kingdom of God would be like if experienced right now, what characteristics would you use to describe that life?

Shalom
Relationship
Intimacy
Life
Freedom
Power
Mission (the missio Dei)

These are realities that God is offering as part of his restoration project that began way back with Abraham. He hasn't given up. Rather, with Jesus, we get a picture and invitation to both the end and the future. Jesus's kingdom is eschatological (the reality of final things as they begin to break in upon God's people) in that it is the culmination of God's invitation to his broken world, but it is still not fully realized until Jesus's final return. So, when we birth communities that are navigating toward true north, we are getting a glimpse of God's divine imagination for his people.

In short, missional communities must create both a context for the divine imagination to be revealed and a place for individuals to be sent into (or live into) the calling God has clearly put on their lives. It is for this reason that we consider ourselves sending communities. Whether being sent across the street or across the world, we are to cultivate leaders who have their finger on the pulse of God's plan for their lives and willingly release them into whatever that plan may be.

So how do we cultivate individuals and communities whose vision is fueled by the divine imagination of God for the advance of his kingdom?

BECOMING A PEOPLE OF VISION

Several years ago, when I was a youth pastor, I remember sitting across from two eighteen-year-old young men who were tired of living stories that didn't have much significance. As they looked into my eyes, I could see their deep longing for something more. Something that required commitment and follow-through. Something that gave them life and brought life to others. I remember thinking that they just needed to get off the couch and begin stepping toward what God was inviting them into.

The sad reality is that a vast number of Christians in the West are terribly bored. Whether they know it or not, our faith has become so domesticated that followers of Jesus really don't know what it means to follow Jesus. To be honest, they don't have to! For the majority of Westerners, we have everything we could possibly want and need. And if we don't have it, we convince ourselves that we need it, and we pour our energy into obtaining it.

When the people of God were in exile at earlier parts in our story, seeking the divine imagination of God was hard to do. Everything around them seemed to be broken, hopeless, and oppressive. Conversely, when we are on the side of the ruling power, divine imagination doesn't seem necessary. There is no sense of urgency driving us toward the heart of God out of hope for our restoration into his kingdom.

Jesus came to proclaim the good news of the kingdom of God through his life, death, and resurrection. This good news calls all of life into submission to his reign. Jesus lives a life of suffering and sacrifice and calls his followers to do the same. Paul says that we are to be imitators of Christ by living cruciform lives—cross-shaped lives that bring about life and hope of the kingdom through sacrifice.

The cruciform life is one that also requires imagination. And unlike idealism, imagination must inform our actions and our way of life. It is not something that is just talked about or even dreamed about: it must be lived out.

I recently had a good friend—a dynamic visionary and teacher—come home in a state of frustration and deep sadness after speaking at a college retreat. He had pushed the young adults to really examine what it would look like to step toward the high calling of Jesus apprenticeship. He had hoped to re-inform their understanding of what it meant to follow Jesus as individuals rooted in the context of community. Although this was a group of longtime Christians, their response was more or less, "We don't have time for that."

I, my friend, and many others would argue that we don't have time to live any other way than in full submission to the cruciform life that requires us to constantly allow the divine imagination of God to realign our ideals. We can so easily settle for second best, third best, or even fourth best when it comes to our understanding of Jesus followership. That simply is not the way God created humanity to live and represent him in the world.

My good friend Nick (or "Big Tex," as he came to be known to us due to his height and Texas roots) recently spent two years in our missional community in Golden Hill, diving deep into our apprenticeship while working a job in construction to make ends meet. Nick lived across the street from my wife and me, along with three other single guys who are part of our community, so one way or another he would end up on our patio a few times a week and we would talk about everything under the sun.

Before he joined our community, Nick had never been in a context in which he was challenged to ask questions and make significant lifestyle choices. He had followed the assumed path of financial and career security that reduced his faith to something that worked alongside his financial and career goals. Nick had an amazing attitude and rarely complained about the life he was living, but he began to ask some hard questions of his assumptions about a year into his time with us. Was he really living out God's calling for his life by aligning with God's kingdom? Was he being fueled by God's imagination for him, or was he being fueled and constrained by his pursuit of financial and vocational security?

As our conversations deepened, it was clear that while Nick wasn't doing anything wrong, neither was he fully living life as it was meant to be lived. In fact, through what we call our Life Compass experience, Nick began to discover that he had a huge heart for justice and community. He was beginning to be captivated not by how much money or power he could accumulate, but by what God had created him to step into as an advocate for the kingdom. It was as if Nick was being freed for the first time to dream alongside God.

This is a picture of what life was meant to be for followers of Jesus. We are free to imagine a new story and are released from the shackles that have been holding us in captivity and keeping us from being fully enlivened participants in the kingdom. To follow Christ is to step out of bondage and into a life and calling that may be misunderstood by many, but is the beginning of a full life of Jesus apprenticeship. It is countercultural, but it is the cruciform life in the kingdom of God.

We are not alone. Multiple times throughout any given month, we have people come live among our community as a stopping place on their pilgrimage toward a new way of participating in kingdom life. Some are simply looking for an open ear while others are actively exploring what it could look like to initiate a similar community in their local context. As we act as a safe harbor for apprentices of Jesus to dream, explore, and experiment, we see that God's imagination is captivating the minds and hearts of his people all over the globe. It is a movement that won't be stopped: it is a movement in which we gladly participate.

BEING A COMMUNITY OF VISION

I don't know how many church board meetings I have sat in throughout the years that were full of amazing people who love God and others, but who failed to create space for the Spirit to re-awaken their churches to the divine imagination. Rather than a posture of anticipation and hope, they adopted a posture of maintenance and preservation, which would often be justified as "good stewardship." This reality debilitates the church, but is also tragic for the advancement of the kingdom. The church must intentionally leave room for burning bushes, rooftop visions, and blinding lights on Damascus roads. It is in those moments of revelation that the divine imagination lifts us from our complacency in order that we might do kingdom work.

In our experience, there is no way to disconnect the imagining process of the community from the imagining process of the individuals who make it up. They are intimately interrelated, and the imagining process can and will shape the life of the community based on what is discerned on the individual level.

Leaving room for the Spirit to initiate these encounters of divine imagination for our lives, we embrace a leadership structure that is built from the bottom up rather than the top down. As individuals in our community discern their calling, our community begins to bend and be shaped around the desires and gifts of those who are a part of our community. Rather than having roles that must be filled by someone, often despite their gifting, we seek to develop roles within our community based on our participants' kingdom calling.

The church ceases to be the church by definition when it is shaped around an organization rather than its members. An organization is an idea or structure. The church is an embodied people who are living on mission, in community, and seeking the guidance of the divine imagination of a God who is ceaselessly working to restore all creation to himself.

Our Integrating and Sustaining Practices

- We use creativity to spark imagination by trying our hand at different art mediums to express ideas. We visit art venues, old and new, to engage our minds and our hearts toward the possibility of something new and creative.
- Each year we take our communities through an extensive process of discerning our unique wiring and the desires God has put on our heart. We paint verbal and visual pictures of the dreams we believe God has for us. We call this process Life Compass, through which we attempt to align our gifts and passions with the mission of God based on the way God has worked in early parts of our individual stories.
- We coach toward our vision statements. In our one-on-one coaching, we help people align their lives with their vision statement. Sometimes it's an affirmation of what they're already living. Other times it's a challenge to live into something different in order to see more of their vision played out in their daily lives.
- We visit places, talk to people, read books, and pursue experiences that will push us outside of what we've only always known and help us imagine another way in God's kingdom.
- We support, partner with, and intentionally learn from others in our city who are progressively addressing issues of injustice.
- We examine our relationships and ask the Holy Spirit to help us imagine a kingdom way in the midst of conflict, stagnancy, and even simple irritation.

- We re-examine our missional engagements and our work, asking the Holy Spirit to give us new ideas for his kingdom to come to those places.
- We immerse ourselves in the book of Acts and reflect on the different ways the Church adapted and created within its culture, listening to God's heart for his Church and his world today.

Missional Possibilities

1. Living out God's sacred imagination is often best expressed when we understand the unique gifts that he has already placed in us. Take some time to pray, asking God for direction, and then make a list of the ways that you have seen God work through you in the past. Sometimes it can be beneficial to ask a few people who know you well to help with this.
2. Write down an Imagination Statement that answers this question: What might God's true north (life as it was meant to be lived) look like if it took place in your life and neighborhood? What things would be different?
3. Considering the gifting that God has placed in you and the vision of transformation expressed in your Imagination Statement, what are some things you can do right away to start to put it into practice? Make a list.

Video Questions

1. What is God calling you to reimagine about your own life? How can living in community strengthen our ability to realize God's mission in and for our individual lives and our unique contexts?

2. How can you begin to recognize the difference between dreaming and imagining and discern God's imagination for your local context?

CHAPTER 6

ENTRUSTING

"'Peace be with you! As the Father has sent me, I am sending you'" (John 20:21).

As I mentioned in Chapter 5, identifying and living into God's imagination really ruined Nick's life. He saw something in himself that connected with the heart of God and his kingdom more intimately than ever before, and he began to wrestle with the implications of taking that seriously.

With his skills in construction, passion for justice, and deep desire to invite others into life in intentional community, Nick was captivated by what our NieuCommunities team in South Africa was doing. He realized he would have the opportunity to use his gift in construction to build in townships that had largely been forgotten in the wake of apartheid. Further, he found out that there was a community of young men who desired to live life in intentional community but had no experience navigating those sometimes-tumultuous waters.

My good friend exchanged the American Dream for the dream of God. God gave him a new imagination for participation in kingdom life, and it was undeniably clear to our community that Nick needed to step into this new chapter of his story. Laying hands on our brother and friend, we blessed and commissioned him as a community in the life and work into which he was faithfully stepping.

The imagining and entrusting postures are intimately connected. When we catch a vision of what God has for his people, we can't help but entrust ourselves to it by stepping forward as sent ones. In this posture, we desire to entrust people to God, celebrate their new or renewed understanding of God's call on their lives, and lean confidently into the future. Without sending, our formation is incomplete: it is where everything falls into place, and it moves us from speaking about it to living it out.

As we enter the path of Jesus, we experience a way forward in which we embrace the formational elements of the monastics while also embracing the missio Dei as has been seen in the missional movements. We are formed and we are sent. It is the only way to fully step into a vocation of Jesus apprenticeship. It is emulating our rabbi.

ACCEPTING THE ROLE OF OUR RABBI

One of Paul's favorite descriptions of Jesus is that of the new Adam. In addition to providing us with insight into the scriptural narrative about which Paul was speaking, it draws some important vocational parallels between Adam and Jesus.

Adam was created to be the mediator between God and creation. He was to represent God's good creation—to steward it faithfully while submitting to the Creator God. Of course, we know there is a break in Adam's faithfulness that leads to a brokenness and disconnection of God from creation.

As the new Adam, Jesus once again stands as the mediator between God and creation. He is a conduit for the restoration agenda that God is putting forth. Unlike the Adam of Genesis, the new Adam remains faithful to both God and creation through his life and ultimate death on a Roman cross. Jesus as the mediator between God and creation is later resurrected and enthroned at the right hand of God as king of the kingdom.

Jesus is faithful in his vocation of mediation, and toward the end of his life and ministry he begins to pass on this vocation of mediation to his disciples. It is not simply a job title; it is the responsibility to carry on the project that was set forth at the beginning of our story. You, I, and all of humanity have been commissioned to represent the restorative love of God to the world and invite them to dance in the rhythms of the creator and redeemer.

With Jesus's enthronement as king of the kingdom, we take on this vocation as mediators and representatives of God's desire and love for creation. As such, we must live as sent ones on mission to represent and restore what God has in mind for the cosmos.

This reality comes to life as Jesus interacts with his disciples in the second part of John's Gospel. Jesus has become the leader and rabbi to a somewhat ragtag bunch of disciples who have followed him all over Palestine. He takes them to places many of them would have never dared wandering through and begins to share a message that radically reorients what it looks like to be a faithful Jew. These ideas are radical, and Jesus's followers have to daily pour their trust into a man who has been captivated by a mission far grander than their imagination would have previously allowed them to navigate.

Imagine following Jesus. Certainly his disciples trust him: he is their leader, after all. Certainly he won't take them into a situation where they are unsafe, right? But then he says, "'As the Father has sent me, I am sending you'" (John 20:21).

The disciples think, "Um, wait. We're on our own? This is obviously an important mission, so why would he leave us?" There is insecurity and fear. But they are not on their own. Jesus tells them that he has offered them the Spirit and that they will do even greater things than he did.

Did they believe that? I don't know. I don't know if I would have. But, if this mission is so important and our leader is passing on the baton to us, we have only one option. Go. Live as sent ones. This is what it means to be a people on mission. We are on the move and participating in the missio Dei. When we have tasted and seen the divine imagination God has for us, we can't help but move.

But being sent isn't just the action we take; it's the posture we adopt in our everyday interactions. It's seeing every experience, conversation, and interaction as an opportunity to participate with God in his restoration project. For me, that looks like being fully present in my conversations with and support of the local farmers' market. It is faithfully stepping into my gifts and calling to write for the benefit of the global church. It is engaging in deep relationships and coaching with those I have chosen to live life with in intentional community. It is advocating and giving a voice to the voiceless through my work in the Middle East. It is celebrating and blessing my wife and daughter whom I have been called to love, serve, and honor.

Finally, it is important to differentiate between being a sent *person* and a sent *people*. God's mission wasn't designed to advance with a set of sent individuals. It was designed to advance through a faithful people living as advocates of the missio Dei. This is why we can't live as sent people alone. It just doesn't work and isn't sustainable. It runs counter to our design and to the ultimate goal of God's redemption project to restore communion with him, his people, and the whole cosmos.

I'm a worse father and husband without a community to encourage, challenge, and partner with me in this sacred devotion. I'm a worse writer without a community that speaks into my work and informs my way forward. Before writing each of these chapters, I sat before a small group of my community mates and sought their advice, insight, and counsel. This is a book about community that was birthed out of community. The longer I live in intentional community, the more I realize I can't see myself or my family living any other way.

ENTRUSTING OURSELVES TO THE MISSION

Ultimately, God is calling his followers to entrust their lives to him. Entrusting is more than offering our lives to God; it is releasing to God and to others the things we hold most dear. As a band of Jesus apprentices who are submerging deep into our local context, we have to daily entrust ourselves, our communities, and our neighborhoods to God. We believe that the only way to be a people of peace is through entrusting ourselves and all of these relationships to the story God is telling all around us.

The idea of holding things loosely enough to keep them fully submitted to the will of God is a radically different paradigm from what is typically being told in the Christian West. Rather than adhering to a narrative of consumption and accumulation, we are pushing toward a narrative of release and multiplication.

Entrusting requires us to be willing to release not just our material resources but also our human resources. I come from a church background that often saw "leaving" a congregation or stepping away from a leadership role for the sake of pursuing God's call on our life as a sign of abandonment. The reason it was seen as abandonment was inherent in the language of leaving. Leaving for the sake of leaving is much, much different from being sent into the story God is telling with your life.

FIELD NOTES: NIEUCOMMUNITIES SAN DIEGO

When I discovered NieuCommunities in 2009 I was going through a tumultuous time in life, and their vision, love, and support came at a time when I deeply needed them. I was so grateful to be invited to join the embodiment of a way of life that sought the kind of integrity that I'd dreamed of and gone around the world in search of for years.

Just as I joined NieuCommunities, the life I'd dedicated to my passion for creation care and social justice received a major blessing. I learned about permaculture, a comprehensive sustainable development system (used by everybody from impassioned activists to NGOs—non-governmental organizations— like Plant With Purpose and World Vision) that cares for the earth and for people more integrally, more holistically, than any other approach I had ever seen. I immediately recognized permaculture as a framework for profoundly missional living, and after taking the standard course to receive my Permaculture Design Certificate (PDC), will be a course assistant next month.

In some ways they recognize and some ways they have yet to, NieuCommunities is heading down the path toward sustainability with much grace. I'm so grateful to have been entrusted and encouraged to begin laying the foundation for a permaculture-themed community that would join NieuCommunities "to shape people and communities to reach beyond the edges of the cultures we know to help re-create a better world," offering our own Permaculture Design Courses and empowering community members to minister more holistically than they ever thought possible.

As I work to build the Missional Permaculture Network International, a platform to connect kingdom-inspired individuals and organizations interested in putting their faith into action using

permaculture, I have been supported and encouraged beyond that which I ever could have imagined.

Our community is consistently creating space for individuals to discern God's imagination for their lives through the context of intentional community. As a result, we have seen God's kingdom breaking through all over the globe as our tribe extends faithfully into their calling. To maintain this reality, we have had to release the expectation of the accumulation of people as we learn to value the reality of the multiplication of our community.

We entrust ourselves to the Spirit's movement in each of our lives because we believe God's kingdom expands through multiplication rather than accumulation. Apprenticing communities that are shaped around life-on-life discipleship can only get so big without losing their apostolic role. Therefore, we seek to ignite a viral movement of missional communities that continue to multiply as people entrust their lives to the work of God.

Not all communities will have this value. Some are called to be communities of apprentices while others are called to be apprenticing communities. There is a distinct different between the two. A community of apprentices is a band of Jesus followers who seek to communally follow Jesus by living missionally every day. An apprenticing community (which has been the historical model of NieuCommunities) is a community that is seeking to intentionally form others toward lives of Jesus apprenticeship with the expectation that they will be sent into something new.

We seek to be a people who embrace a DNA of missional life that inherently invites others into the missio Dei. It's not simply about being good news in our daily interactions at the park with a group of young moms, but about inviting them into the way of Jesus, which leads to intentional apprenticeship. We are to reproduce leaders in ways that are similar to how we have been led. And as we entrust what we have learned and experienced to others, we delight in a divine chain reaction that leaves our world a better place as God's will is done on earth as it is in heaven.

ENTRUSTING EMBODIED

Deep Surrender

Ali is my good friend and one of my heroes. He has taught me so much. Ali grew up a Shi'ite Muslim in Iran. In an effort to complete his studies as a doctor of neurology, he moved to the United States about three years ago. His whole life is in Iran—family, religion, tradition, friends, and home.

After moving to New Orleans, Ali met Matt and Amy, one of the couples who are now on staff with our NieuCommunities team in San Diego. Although coming from two very different backgrounds (Iran and Washington State), they immediately connected and became close friends. More than anything, Ali became intrigued by this Jesus around whom their lives revolved. Within his Muslim tradition, Jesus is a prominent and highly respected prophet, but to believe in him as God is to commit *shirk* (holding anything/anyone as equal with Allah/God), the worst sin of all.

Ali became so intrigued by the Jesus he saw in his friends that when they moved to San Diego to go on staff with NieuCommunities, he asked if he could come with them and be a part of our missional community. So, Ali found a neurology position in San

Diego, packed his bags, and moved not just to San Diego, but into our neighborhood of Golden Hill.

It is there that I met one of the most brilliant, yet humble and devoted men I have ever encountered. As a doctor, Ali's work was frequently published in highly respected medical journals. His devotion and dedication also extended beyond his profession: he set aside three times in his day to pray out of devotion and reverence. Anytime I saw him pray, no matter the setting, he would turn his palms face up as if opening and surrendering himself to whatever God was speaking. For Ali, presence and devotion to his faith could be second to nothing, and his life reflected that.

Although he was a brilliant doctor and had been devoted to Islam, Ali was a humble learner who made the most of every opportunity to hear and experience the Jesus of his friends. Ali dove deep into our Christian community as he prayed, worshiped, listened, and practiced beside us. He wanted to encounter Jesus, so he chose to submerge himself into a band of believers who were submitting their lives to their king.

Ali became a very good friend of mine. I have spent a lot of time studying Islam as I seek to engage people like Ali and develop my role as peacemaker in the Middle East conflicts. Despite my occasional ignorance, Ali would listen to my questions and share insight into his sacred traditions. He once told the Yackleys and Chapmans (housemates who typically hosted our worships gatherings and a number of other community parties) that he "felt like he was at mosque" when he was in their home.

Ali became my friend and dialogue partner in the areas we each held most sacred. It wasn't a competition for whose religion was more "right." Instead, it was a dialogue of mutual respect and reverence. He wanted to experience the truth of Jesus, and he asked that we intercede on his behalf. Through the lives and worship of his new friends and the profound work of the Spirit, my friend Ali did encounter Jesus in his time here in Golden Hill. After a recent worship gathering, Ali looked at me and said, "Yes, I am a follower of Jesus."

Just a few months ago, Ali accepted a position at Temple University in Philadelphia and moved away from his new family in Golden Hill. While it was hard for us to say goodbye, both Ali and our community knew this was not the end of our story together. On the day he left, we took Ali surfing for the first time then gathered for a meal. We shared the ways he had impacted us and thanked him for all that he had taught us. He came to us as a student, but his humble devotion taught us so much.

Before Ali walked out the door to catch his flight, we all turned our palms to the sky and thanked Jesus for our friend, our brother. Ali was not moving for a random job across the country. He was being sent by a community that was entrusting their friend to the call God had put on his life. Ali was going exactly where he needed to go and we were right alongside him in this new chapter of his kingdom adventure.

Missionary Redefined

Adrienne was raised in a missionary family in South America and had spent her adult life in Colombia doing extremely difficult mission work. As a result, she joined our community in South Africa pretty beat up. She was physically tired, disillusioned, and struggling to connect everyday life and work with her role in God's mission.

During her year apprenticing with our team in the context of intentional community, she was loved well and listened to but was also given a context to explore what it was God had really put on her heart to do and be as a kingdom participant. She was given the freedom and place to dream and begin to integrate her gifting with everyday mission.

After reading Julie Cameron's *The Artist's Way: A Spiritual Path to Higher Creativity* as a community, Adrienne's long suppressed creativity began to be unearthed. She discovered that she had a passion to capture the life and movement of God's creation through photography. She found great joy in this practice, but more than that, she discovered her work as a photographer didn't have to be separate from her "mission" as an apprentice of Jesus. At the end of her time with our community, she was affirmed in her gifting and sent into her calling as a photographer for the good of the kingdom.

Urban Garden

Our missional community in Vancouver started a community garden in their neighborhood as a way to faithfully steward creation and create a context for missional interaction with their neighbors.

The project immediately took off and our team took a leading role at the intersection of ecology and the church in that region. As part of their weekly rhythms, apprentices would work in the garden while also cultivating new friendships that otherwise may never have come to life. The garden became their baby, and they took great responsibility to care for its life and the life of the new relationships that began to sprout as a result.

Over time, a local church became increasingly supportive of the project. After much thought, prayer, and conversation, our team decided to entrust this rich asset to another community of faith that would have the capacity to enhance what had taken root. Our community had put in the effort, both physically and relationally, but they knew that in entrusting it to others, it would be best used for the kingdom.

BEING SENT TO OUR NEIGHBORHOODS

As I have said, being sent doesn't necessarily mean doing something different or moving across the word or country. In entrusting ourselves to God and his mission, we choose to live as a sent people every day, in every interaction and activity. Being a sent people means that we view what in the past may have seemed mundane or normal as a potential opportunity for God's kingdom to be made real, for heaven and earth to be only thinly separated.

As I mentioned earlier, Jon and Sophia Hall opened Make Good with the hopes of building relationships with neighbors, building a voice in the art scene of San Diego, and offering economic opportunities to those who otherwise wouldn't have any. This project was birthed out of the divine imagination God had for their lives, and they have, in faithfulness, chosen to live as "sent people" in this important work.

What would happen if all of God's people began to ask, *How can I engage my neighborhood as a "sent one?"*

Shortly after moving into Golden Hill, our community began to ask this question and started experimenting. Over the years, thin places have been budding out of the unique soil of our neighborhood. We have simply chosen to get dirty, to submerge into this soil and begin to sow seeds of hope, transformation, and renewal out of our desire to faithfully live as apprentices of Jesus.

Entrusting our lives to God requires that we view all of life as an opportunity to be a "sent people." As followers of Jesus, living as a sent people becomes a vocational mandate. We can no longer settle for simply "going" to church on Sunday or helping out at an outreach event. Those aren't bad things, but they are at best a fractured semblance of the beautiful picture God is painting in and through our lives—lives that we must be willing to entrust fully to the story he is telling.

We may be sent across the world as we unearth the imagination God has for our lives. But, more likely, and undoubtedly in this moment, we are all called to live as sent ones in our neighborhoods, families, and schools. As a missional-monastic community, we are fueled by the missio Dei and enlivened by the Spirit that is at work inside and all around us.

As a community, we must go. We must turn off our TVs. We must shut off our computers. We must begin to spend less time inside the four walls of our church buildings.

It is time to inhabit the places where life is being lived. In the parks. In the community centers. Under highway overpasses. In local businesses. At farmers' markets. In the home of the single mom on your block.

It is in being fully present in these places and fully expectant that the Spirit is at work that we experience heaven crashing into earth—a thin place.

Our Integrating and Sustaining Practices

Chaz and David have made their dream of starting a community soccer league a reality. They posted ads on Craigslist and began to invite their neighbors. Within a few months, they had more than thirty people gathering each week to play indoor soccer at our Golden Hill community center.

Rebecca postures herself as a sent one by extending into deep relationships with women in the CRASH halfway home I mentioned earlier.

Maria mentors women in their homes throughout our neighboring city of Tijuana.

Carli and my wife, Jan, live as sent ones as they build relationships with refugees who have escaped persecution and are now living in San Diego and trying to reassemble their lives without any security of home (culturally, geographically, and so on). Although most of the refugees adhere to different religions, these faithful women embody the heart of Jesus through play, sincere listening, and endless love for people who have otherwise been largely deprived of it.

Molly is a gifted musician who uses her unique platform to live as a sent one by extending and participating in the story of God through her art.

Max works as an advocate and representative of local Boy Scouts and has relationally extended into the fabric of families and subcultures that otherwise wouldn't be inhabited with the good news of Jesus.

Todd and David spend time each week developing and growing in their relationships with friends who find themselves living on the streets and in their cars. In the sacramental act of a shared meal, they enter into the stories of those who otherwise are forgotten and neglected by society.

Laurie spends her Saturday mornings participating in Zumba at the local Spanish-speaking church alongside dozens of women whose lives would otherwise not intersect.

Jan, Jenna, Rebecca, Melissa, and Amy mentor local teenage girls who have suffered through extreme poverty or family breakdown. Under the warm sun, these young girls circle the table on our patio and share laughter, experiences, and intimate stories with women who want nothing more than to be a presence of peace in their otherwise tumultuous lives.

Matt and Rob coached basketball at the local High School and helped shaped the life trajectory of both players and coaches.

Holly left her secure job in the suburbs to move into the neighborhood and pursue her speech therapy profession on a more limited basis in order to give more of her life to her community.

Peter had a seemingly dry plot of dirt in front of his apartment that he has chosen to turn into a community urban garden. Neighbors now look out their second-story windows down at the fertile garden and ask how they can be part of it. Peter is creating an opportunity for people to commune and find life among the creation to which God so intimately tied us.

Shaun effortlessly turns daily chores into opportunities to make new friends and immediately encourage them through intentional acts of kindness.

As a community, we make time to bless, encourage, and pray for those who are leaving us to pursue the call of God on their life. This has taken place at our Sunday gatherings, farewell/sending parties, or shared meals. We practice this with those who are being sent from us but also with other brothers and sisters who are passing through. Like the believers at Antioch did with Paul, we speak words of exhortation, tell them what we see in them, and pray over them. It's always a beautiful time.

Missional Possibilities

1. When you come "palms up" before God, to what do you hear God entrusting you? What steps can you take to explore and discover what lies in that direction?
2. Who is someone in your faith community moving in a God direction? How can you encourage them? What would it look like to "entrust" them in that direction?
3. Who is someone you want to get to know better and encourage in his or her journey with Christ? What is something "for the good of your city" that you could do together?

Video Questions

1. Why do you think leaving (in the Christian context) has had such a negative connotation? What can we do to transform leaving to sending, to let those who leave us "go with not just grace but celebration?"
2. Why are we sometimes scared to entrust ourselves to God's provision when he sends us? How can we encourage members of our community to entrust themselves to God and his mission?

AFTERWORD

These postures and the stories that fill them out aren't concrete, sure-fire steps to a vibrant life as a missional community. They are simply field notes from our humble attempts at living out the mission of God in the context of covenant community. It is messy, it is discouraging, but it is beautiful and I really, really think it is worth a shot.

Janna, a midwife at a local birthing center where a few of the babies in our community were born (including our little daughter, Ruby), made a sign of a cross and prayed a quick blessing over Derek and Christiana's daughter, Anika, moments after she was born. Both the parents were deeply moved by this sincere act of love and care.

Over the course of the next year, Janna became close friends with Christiana and many of the other women in our community. Soon, it was Janna's turn to get pregnant and embrace the sacred anticipation of new life and an expanding family.

A few months into her pregnancy, Janna's husband broke relationship with her and their quickly developing child. She was crushed and struggled to see the baby's pending arrival as a blessing. Feeling alone, abandoned, and heartbroken, our little tribe of Jesus apprentices began to surround her with love that she desperately needed during this vulnerable time.

Helping her find an apartment in our neighborhood, we moved Janna into our "home" just weeks before the baby was due. All the moms excitedly got her fully equipped with hand-me-downs and threw an incredible baby shower.

Committed to natural childbirth, Janna decided to have a homebirth in her apartment and asked Rebecca and Christiana to be in on the labor as doulas. After forty-three hours of hard labor, Janna gave birth to a healthy baby boy. Having not yet decided on a name, she temporarily called her new little companion "Turkey."

Reflecting on the impact Janna's blessing had made on her and Derek, Christiana asked if we could come over and pray a blessing over Janna and Turkey. Just twenty-four hours after the birth, our tribe filled her little apartment and prayed blessings over Janna and her precious little boy.

With tears filling her eyes, Janna looked down at her son and said, "This is the village I have been telling you about."

We were no longer just Janna's friends: we had become her village, her community.

When she said these words, I was stirred to tears. This was what it is all about. This was the way God had created his community to function. God's dreams for his people were being made real in this small apartment in Golden Hill. It truly was a thin place.

Two of my closest friends have followed (from afar) the life we now live as part of NieuCommunities. They have offered endless support, but they have also asked the hard questions that have led me to deeper conviction in our calling to live in missional community. Within the course of the same week, they each separately said, "The ministry you're in and the life you're living give me hope that my ideals for the church can become reality."

My response was brief: "Please know that they can be."

Life on mission in the context of intentional community is not a far-out ideal: it is a reality waiting for others to step into. Consider joining me. Consider joining us in the global movement that is seeking to faithfully tell God's story.

APPENDIX

NieuCommunities' Covenant

A covenant is a commitment made within the context of relationship. It's a commitment to act in certain ways, and in our case, to be a certain kind of people. It's a commitment that deeply connects us to one another and unites us around a shared calling.

Our covenant is a collective covenant, which means we are together declaring our intentions. The covenant expresses what we are committed to do and be, collectively. We recognize that people are at different stages in life and will participate in the community at varying depths. We also know that none of us will ever do this perfectly. But all of us who covenant to be part of this community are doing our best to align our lives with these commitments.

Our covenant is rooted in our three core commitments. It describes how we, in our various locations, will pursue our calling to be a mentoring and sending community that develops people to live missional lives wherever God calls them.

The NieuCommunities Common Covenant

Communion

We believe that we were created to be worshipers and lovers of God.

As such, we will make the Triune God the center of our lives by collectively and individually committing to live as disciples of Christ.

This includes cultivating an attitude of thankfulness, a lifestyle of prayer and worship, a deep and responsive engagement with Scripture, a reliance on the provision and guidance of the Holy Spirit, exploring and practicing a diversity of spiritual disciplines, discovering God's goodness and beauty in his created world, and the intentional participation in the gift of Sabbath.

Community

We believe that the Gospel is best experienced and expressed within a community of Christ-followers.

Because of this, we will open our lives to be shaped by the community in which God has placed us.

Our journey together will include living in the same neighborhood, opening our lives and homes as places of invitation and hospitality, gathering at least once a week over a common meal, caring for and submitting to one another, speaking well of one another and defending each other's names, sharing stories and reflecting on God's work of love in our midst, living more simply and sharing our resources with those in need, and gathering together weekly to grow and to be formed as apprentices of Jesus.

Context

We believe that God calls all followers of Christ to live a life of mission.

In obedience to this, we will incarnate the good news of the kingdom and become a reconciling and redemptive presence in the places we inhabit.

This life of mission will include "submerging" in our own unique neighborhood, living as the light of God's grace in places of darkness, inviting neighbors and friends to experience a different kind of faith community, becoming true caretakers of God's creation, creating spaces and moments for our neighbors to experience both community and communion with God, discipling our neighbors into deeper relationship with Jesus, partnering with other leaders in our city to advance the kingdom, helping to birth new faith communities, and apprenticing young leaders to live out all of these things with us and wherever God sends them.

NOTES

Introduction

1. Jurgen Moltmann, *The Church in the Power of the Spirit: A Contribution to Messianic Ecclesiology*, London: SCM Press, 1977, 64.

2. Ibid.

3. Christopher J. H. Wright, *The Mission of God: Unlocking the Bible's Grand Narrative,* Downer's Grove, IL: IVP Academic, 2006, 23.

4. Ibid, 22.

5. Ibid.

6. Dr. Feldmeth, Lecture, "The Development and Impact of Monasticism," Fuller Theological Seminary. Fall 2010.

7. Kenneth S. Latourette, *A History of Christianity Volume 1: to A.D. 1500*, New York: HarperCollins, 1953, 226.

8. Ibid, 228.

9. Ibid, 227.

10. George G. Hunter, III, *The Celtic Way of Evangelism: How Christianity Can Reach the West . . . Again*, Nashville, TN: Abingdon Press, 2000, 27.

11. Ibid.

12. Ibid, 28.

13. J. R. Daniel Kirk, *Jesus Have I Loved, But Paul?: A Narrative Approach to the Problem of Pauline Christianity*, Grand Rapids, MI: Baker Academic, 2011, 57.

14. Ibid, 72.

Chapter 1

1. Wendell Berry, *Leavings: Poems*, Berkeley, CA: Counterpoint Press, 2010, 84.

2. The Radical Reformation came about as a result of the Reformation that was led by Luther and Calvin. Radical Reformers didn't believe that the Reformers took the life and teaching of Jesus seriously enough and began a movement whose ethic and way of life were shaped by Jesus's teaching in the Sermon on the Mount. Specifically emphasizing the value of community, simplicity, and nonviolence, the Anabaptist tradition was birthed within the Radical Reformation.

3. Stanley J. Grenz, *Theology for the Community of God*, Grand Rapids, MI: Wm. B. Eerdmans, and Regent College Publishing: Vancouver, 2000, 24. Copyright 1994 by Broadman & Holman Publishers.

4. Robin Mass and Gabriel O'Donnell, *Spiritual Traditions for the Contemporary Church*. Nashville, TN: Abingdon Press, 1990, 76.

5. Mark Scandrette recently gave this analogy while spending a couple days with our community.

6. Parker Palmer, *Let Your Life Speak: Listening for the Voice of Vocation*, San Francisco: Jossey-Bass, 2000, 4-5.

7. If you don't have the videos but would like to purchase them in the Small Group Edition, go to thehousestudio.com.

Chapter 2

1. Jer Swigart said this while we were sitting over a meal in San Francisco a few months ago. He is a Pastor at the Open Door Community, a community that is trying to cultivate Jesus followers who are radically submerged in their local contexts and neighborhoods.

2. I learned this history from Dr. Robert Mullins while studying in Israel in 2010. Jerusalem University College, Galilee Field Study Lecture.

Chapter 3

1. Christine Pohl, *Making Room: Recovering Hospitality as a Christian Tradition*, Grand Rapids, MI: Wm. B. Eerdmans, 1999, 169.

2. Philip Freeman, *St. Patrick of Ireland: A Biography*. New York: Simon and Schuster, 2004, 40.

3. Ibid, 50.

4. Ibid, 73.

5. Thomas Cahill, *How the Irish Saved Civilization: The Untold Story of Ireland's Heroic Role from the Fall of Rome to the Rise of Medieval Europe*, New York: Anchor, 1996, 156.

6. Ibid, 159.

7. Dietrich Bonhoeffer, *The Cost of Discipleship*. Translated from the German *Nachfolge*, first published in 1937 by Chr. Kaiser Verlag München. SCM Press, 1959.

Chapter 4

1. Permaculture (a conjunction of *permanent* and *culture)* is a holistic sustainable design founded in the 1970s on the three ethics of earth care, people care and fair share.

2. John Goldingay, *Old Testament Theology: Israel's Gospel (Vol. 1)*, Downer's Grove, IL: InterVarsity Press, 2003, 348.

3. Ibid, 349.

4. J. R. Daniel Kirk, *Jesus Have I Loved, But Paul?: A Narrative Approach to the Problem of Pauline Christianity*, Grand Rapids, MI: Baker Academic, 2011, 54.

5. Ibid.

6. We acknowledge and thank John Reed, Pastor at TerraNova Church, who shared these patterns in a sermon

7. Dietrich Bonhoeffer, *Life Together: The Classic Exploration of Faith in Community*, New York: Harper & Row, 1954, 116.

8. Jean Vanier, *Community and Growth*, New York: Paulist Press, 1989, 102. Originally published as *La Communauté: Lieu du Pardon et de la Fête* by Les Editions Fleurus, Paris.

Chapter 5

1. Wendell Berry, *Standing by Words: Essays*, Berkeley, CA: Counterpoint, 1983, 90.

2. Dallas Willard, *The Divine Conspiracy: Rediscovering Our Hidden Life in God*, New York: HarperCollins, 1998, 25.